MW01279857

Madison Career Learning Center
P.O. Box 27
Madison, SD 57042

DEADLY REUNION

DEADLY REUNION

JAN EKSTRÖM

Translated by
JOAN TATE

CHARLES SCRIBNER'S SONS · NEW YORK

Copyright © 1975 Jan Ekström
English translation Copyright © 1982 by Charles Scribner's Sons

Ättestupan, published by Bonniers, Stockholm, 1975
First published in the United States
in translation from the Swedish
by Charles Scribner's Sons, 1983

Library of Congress Cataloging in Publication Data

Ekström, Jan, 1923–
Deadly reunion.
Translation of: Ättestupan.
I. Title.
PT9876.15.K74A9   1983   839.7'374   82-10455
ISBN 0-684-17765-X

This book published simultaneously
in the United States of America and in Canada—
Copyright under the Berne Convention.

1 3 5 7 9 11 13 15 17 19   F/C   20 18 16 14 12 10 8 6 4 2
Printed in the United States of America.

THE FAMILY

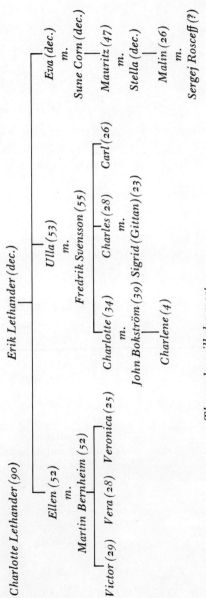

Charlotte Lethander (90)
Erik Lethander (dec.)

Ellen (52)
m.
Martin Bernheim (52)

Ulla (53)
m.
Fredrik Svensson (55)

Eva (dec.)
m.
Sune Corn (dec.)

Mauritz (47)
m.
Stella (dec.)

Malin (26)
m.
Sergej Rosceff (?)

Victor (29)   Vera (28)   Veronica (25)

Charlotte (34)
m.
John Bokström (39)   Sigrid (Gittan) (23)   Charles (28)
m.
Carl (26)

Charlene (4)

The reader will also meet

Melander, Chief of Police in the district
Bertil Durell, Police Inspector

Alma Gren, housekeeper to Miss Lethander
Lucy, Miss Lethander's cat

DEADLY
REUNION

1

ULLA

THE LUNCH WAS COMING TO AN END. THE CHAIR ON OLD Aunt Lethander's left was still empty, but apart from that the whole family was there, arranged around the long oval table like board members of a giant corporation. But not exactly. They were seated alternately male and female, and the average age was rather low. Miss Lethander's made up for that somewhat. Her ninetieth birthday was coming up.

There was certainly no enthusiasm in the atmosphere. The food had been fine: hot dishes, cold dishes, smoked eel as thick as a salami, herring, and omelets of various sorts—cauliflower, ham, clam and shrimp, and, of course, chanterelle mushroom. But the drinks had been poor: milk, beer, and fruit juice. Ulla knew that Fredrik was suffering. Still, she thought that it was stupid of him to hint that the food needed something to cut the oiliness, for Aunt Lethander might realize that he never ate eel without a couple of drinks along with it. There was no need to annoy Aunt Charlotte.

Fredrik was sitting a long way down the table, counting away from Aunt Charlotte. The Bernheim sisters flanked him —Vera on his right, Veronica on his left. Ulla noticed this with a certain disquietude. She had made a careful study of where everyone was placed in relation to Miss Lethander, since she had a vague feeling that the seating plan mirrored the old woman's likes and dislikes. With a great deal of mental effort she had tried to work out a sort of point system that would clarify matters.

There were fifteen people at the table, not counting Miss Lethander. The empty chair, on which the cat had settled as soon as Miss Lethander sat down, would count as seven points, as would Martin Bernheim's place. He was sitting on Miss Lethander's other side, with herself, Ulla, as dining partner. That gave her a six, just balanced by Ellen Bernheim, who was sitting in a comparable position on the other side of the table. Then, thank god, came Carl, with five points, as opposed to Malin Rosceff's five, and then on the other side young Charlotte and Charles, both with four. Victor and Vera Bernheim could be counted as three points each. My god, how far down Fredrik was sitting. Only two points at most, and the same for Gittan.

How could Aunt Charlotte have been so filthy as to give only a two to a gorgeous girl like Gittan? Especially when she hadn't met her before. Well, there was one consolation— Veronica Bernheim was just as far down the table (two points), and that foreigner, Malin's husband, was lucky to get a single point.

Ulla became carried away by her calculations. First, she tried to add the family points in her head. All the Bernheims together. Then her own family—herself, Fredrik, Charles, Carl, young Charlotte, and John—what a shame that little Charlene was too young to be at the table—and then the Rosceffs. But there were too many figures and she kept having to go back to check her allotment of points. She drew a deep breath and took a sausage and a meatball to help her. The sausage was her family, the Svenssons, and the meatball the Bernheims. She could leave the Rosceffs out, since they had no chance to win.

She cut the sausage and meatball into small bits and pushed them around her plate to correspond to the seating plan. Then she discreetly moved over a slice of cucumber to stand for Aunt Charlotte and began to calculate. Twenty-six for the Bernheims and, thank god, twenty-eight for the Svenssons. But then a horrible thought struck her. The Svenssons were ahead in total points, but the points might have to be averaged out per person. There was one more Svensson than Bernheim—no, *two* more—she had completely forgotten John. That would bring the Svensson average down below the Bernheim. She now gave up in confusion when she realized that her bits of sausage and meatball could not contend with the new factor.

She was suddenly aware that a dead silence had fallen around the table, and she darted a glance around to see the reason for it. It was Aunt Charlotte. And she herself, for Aunt Charlotte was staring right at her. As their eyes met, the old woman said, "Don't you like the food, Ulla?"

"Oh, certainly, of course. I was just thinking."

"Then don't sit there picking at it like a bird. And don't push your cucumber away. Cucumbers are good for you. They may not have vitamins, but they have minerals."

Aunt Charlotte obviously expected Ulla to start eating, and Ulla nervously picked up the slice of cucumber on her fork and put it in her mouth. As she ate it the thought came into her mind, My god, did she mean something by that? Had she figured out that Ulla was using the slice of cucumber to stand for her and was now chewing her up—which, naturally, she should not do? Or, eat me and you get minerals. Yes, of course, minerals—that could mean money. That's the kind of nasty dig that Aunt Charlotte is famous for. Ulla looked away. She knew that she was blushing from nervousness and she looked helplessly around the table for support. Then she discovered that something was really going on.

Charles was sitting opposite her, to her right. He had set down his knife and fork, though his plate was still heaped with mushroom omelet, his favorite dish. He was staring, as if he had had a stroke, across the table at Gittan, his wife, who was sitting beside Victor Bernheim. Ulla turned her head. It was with a sense of shock that she saw that Victor was holding Gittan's head between his hands and pressing a kiss on her lips. Gittan let him do it without protesting. At that moment Charles's paralysis vanished, and he got up so violently that the chinaware on the table jumped and clinked, a glass was overturned, and his chair crashed over behind him. Old Miss Lethander was watching him with interest.

"What the hell is going on?" he shouted. He seized the edge of the table and leaned forward as if he were going to hurl himself across it. His hands were white, his face beet red, and his hair wild.

Victor released Gittan's blond head. His eyes were shining. He leaned back, took a fork, and, tapping it against the edge of his plate, sang the three immortal words of the Beatles, "Love, love, love."

Then he began to eat again, as if nothing had happened. But Charles remained standing, his eyes glistening with rage.

Ulla held her breath. Why didn't Fredrik do something? She looked around. Why didn't anyone do anything? They were all looking at Charles, almost in expectation, as if they hoped that he would pick up a plate or the pitcher of fruit juice and throw it in Victor's face. That would be a catastrophe. That would alienate Aunt Charlotte forever.

Ulla tried to catch Charles's eye. She lifted her hand in a vague way and waved with her fingers for him to sit down again. And the miracle happened. Nothing was thrown. Instead he turned around, picked up his chair, and sat down again. But Ulla did not feel secure until he had pushed his first forkful of omelet into his mouth.

Aunt Charlotte had not shown any particular reaction. Actually, she had looked a little amused. Nor had Gittan forgotten herself and given Victor a wallop on the head or anything of the sort. She just smiled. Perhaps she was a little flushed, but all through Victor's escapade she had acted as if it had nothing to do with her. Ulla felt a certain reluctant admiration and whispered to Martin Bernheim, "Didn't she really have self-control and class?"

4

This episode was one of the events during the luncheon. How Aunt Charlotte had taken it was hard for Ulla to decide. To no one's advantage, probably; to the disadvantage of both, possibly, but more to Victor's, since he had started things.

The other event was the picture taking. Ulla had not anticipated the muttered insults and the sarcastic taunts between the heads of the various families, nor the offensive grimaces and insinuations. Nor had she expected that old Aunt Charlotte would remain silent (until her moment came).

Yes, the other event was the picture taking. It took place before they sat down at table. It was Ellen Bernheim's idea, and Victor who took the pictures. "He's a first-rate photographer," Ellen said, "and since he has his camera with him . . ."

Oh, yes. Ulla had heard that Victor took photographs. But she understood that they were of naked women and that he used to sell them to certain dubious girlie magazines. She wondered if Ellen knew about it, for then she wouldn't have been so eager to play up her son's hobby. After all, no one seemed to have any enthusiasm about the photos. Except Aunt Charlotte. But that settled the matter and no one raised any objections.

Victor took a great many photographs. The flashes dazzled Ulla's sensitive eyes again and again, and were reflected painfully from the long mirrors that covered the dining-room wall opposite the row of windows. It all gave Ulla a slight headache, which kept recurring throughout the lunch. But the photographs also gave her something else to think about. What was it all about? An uncomfortable feeling for Ulla. Did Ellen have a definite purpose when she arranged for the picture taking?

While she was thinking about it Ulla positioned herself diagonally in front of Fredrik, with Lucy, the cat, in her arms. She knew that Aunt Lethander thought people should be fond of animals. So she had seized the cat before anyone else thought of it. She didn't mind that the cat had scratched her hands a little, and now it was lying quietly, like a baby, in her arms. Thank heaven, she should say, for Aunt Lethander had seen her and given her a friendly smile, which Ulla answered by carefully stroking the cat along its soft back.

After the first flash she turned her head a little and whispered to her husband, "Who's going to get any pleasure out of these pictures?"

He whispered back, "There's something behind it!"

"Can't you at least look pleasant and smile, Fredrik?"

He answered by jabbing her in the side with his elbow, partly to show her that he didn't like what was going on, partly to quiet her. So she said nothing more, but listened to an interesting point of view from Carl, who was standing next to her.

Fredrik whispered, "Don't look so pleased. I'll bet the old hag just wants a good picture of the chief mourners."

Fredrik had not been discreet enough. The others—Gittan, young Charlotte, and Vera, the older of the Bernheim girls—started to giggle. Ulla cast a frightened glance at Aunt Lethander, but the small, translucent face under its frame of silvery hair revealed nothing. Whether she had heard or not.

"But it was Ellen who wanted it," muttered Fredrik.

When Victor was finished with the photographs, Aunt Charlotte crossed over to the table and placed herself behind each chair in turn. "Martin, will you sit here? Ulla, will you sit here? Carl, you here . . ." One after another until all the places were allocated. All but one.

The empty chair was on Aunt Charlotte's left. Ulla had a good idea for whom it was intended. Mauritz. But Mauritz had not put in his appearance yet.

Then the food was brought in. Alma directed the serving girls from the neighboring farm with quiet, precise motions. This dish there, the carrots there, the herring to Miss Lethander and then pass it around. If they wanted anything else, she would be in the kitchen. And then came Ulla's somewhat confused attempt to work out points and the interlude with Charles. Then the plates were empty, and Alma and her girls came back and started to clear the table. Veronica and Vera Bernheim got up and helped, and Ulla leaped to her feet so that there would be no risk of losing points. To her great satisfaction, young Charlotte also helped without being asked. They all sat down at the table again with their coffee before them, and then came old Miss Lethander's moment.

She got up from the table and stood behind her chair. It was a high-backed chair that almost blocked her from view. All that could be seen of her—above the cushion, which was embroidered with petit point, and the carved mahogany frame—was her head and shoulders. Her white hair looked like a thin summer cloud above the sky of her light blue, high-necked dress. She let her gaze wander around the table, where all were sitting in silence, waiting for her to begin.

And speak she did, in her usual formal manner. For Ulla, the beginning was magnificent.

"I care very much for my family. I care very much for all of you . . ."

This second statement was perhaps a suspicion too broad. It implied a zero position, a position of equality for everyone. It also suggested ingratitude, considering all the efforts that Ulla had made over the years to be liked a *little* more than the others around the table. Aunt Charlotte's next statements awakened new expectations.

"Still, one cannot help having favorites. It is human. Indeed, it is not only human, it is inevitable, as long as people have different attitudes toward you. One might well say that affection fosters affection."

Ulla let her breath out. Aunt Charlotte had observed and taken note. Ulla even thought that the old lady let her eyes rest on her and her children a little longer than on the others. What a blessed inspiration it had been to name the children with a hint—no, not a hint—Ulla sought feverishly for a better word—a sign, a token, a *demonstration*—of her affection. When she and Fredrik had used Aunt Lethander's name, Charlotte, as a model for the names of the children

7

and their grandchild: Charlotte, Charles, Carl, Charlene. A real proof of affection.

Ulla swallowed nervously when she suddenly realized that Aunt Charlotte had paused for a long time. Then the old woman continued. "By affection, naturally, I do not mean fawning or currying favor. I am well aware that I am rich. When people go past, they say, 'In that house up there lives the richest old hag in the district.' And that includes factory owners and big businessmen. Oh, yes. I know only too well that I have money. I also know that one or two of you here at this table entertain hopes of getting part of it when I'm gone. But fawning or currying favor will not give you any advantage."

Ulla's heart leaped. Fawning? Currying favor? She couldn't have meant that naming the children was fawning, could she? She looked tensely at Aunt Charlotte and what she feared most happened. The old woman looked back at her coldly, with a coldness, Ulla thought, that cut through flesh and nerves and with its icy tip punctured a great rosy hope.

Ulla could not breathe. Perhaps she was too sensitive— perhaps she was misinterpreting. She was able to breathe again when she saw the look continue on around the table, from face to face, resting on Ellen Bernheim at least as long as it had on her. *She*, Ellen Bernheim, certainly could be accused of currying favor. The eggs. Hadn't she brought with her a basket of eggs so full that it was a miracle that they weren't smashed into an omelet in the basket? And speaking of omelets—Charles's had been made with mushrooms, his favorite, and Fredrik's with shrimp. Wasn't that as good a sign as anything?

Aunt Charlotte continued. "No, currying favor will not create any advantage. But I also believe that I am old and wise enough not to *exclude* anyone for it. I know only too well that you all put on happy faces and try to be friendly to me so that you won't lose anything by default. It doesn't cost you any great effort, since we meet so seldom." She looked at Ulla again. "A Christmas card. A vacation card from Majorca from Charles. All surely inspired by Ulla's kind consideration . . ."

Ulla felt her heart jump again. Was that sarcasm or was it meant literally? But she must know that Ulla, nearly all her life, had genuinely felt a—she was looking for the exact word again—motivating force, a compulsion to think of her old aunt. Often. She could swear that it was disinterested. It was just there. Some diffuse process in her heart that produced this feeling, which she had never bothered to analyze. You couldn't call it love or family feeling, but, well, attachment, reverence, respect for a rich old—no, not that—a wise old human being.

"I said just now that some of the people in this area refer to me as an old hag. Indeed, some of you in this immediate area do the same."

There was another pause. Ulla suddenly felt that everything was tumbling down into an abyss. This was all the result of Fredrik's unforgivable remark when Victor was taking pictures. Aunt Charlotte had heard it. Or someone else had heard it and told her, someone who knew how to turn a casual, unguarded remark to his or her own advantage. No affection in the world could compensate for such an insulting act of stupidity. Everything went empty inside Ulla. All her work had been in vain, just because of that one word. She would have forgiven him if he had only thought it and not said it. Aunt Charlotte fixed her gaze on Fredrik. Fredrik met her glance without turning red or even looking as if he took the remark as meant for him. Or even understood it. Well, that might be sensible. And yet . . . Aunt Charlotte knew. It did not help trying to look innocent.

"I wish that there were more of this. Not that I like the word, but I respect the honesty. It is straight and honest to say what you think, even if you do offend the old hag, and not to care how much money she might leave you."

These words seemed like a spring breeze to Ulla. They

slipped into her ears and brought everything back to life. Dear Fredrik. She looked tenderly at him. Big, heavy, and red-faced, he sat there, an incorruptible ally, fearless and honorable, straight and honest. No fawning or flattery. He said just what he thought and that is what he has always done. She felt her own lips forming the word—hag, hag—and then, with frightened delight—bitch of an old hag. Yes, he sometimes said that, too, when talking about Aunt Charlotte.

"Nevertheless, I have not had much confidence in all of you when it came to money and my property. There has been only one of you on whom I could completely rely."

Ulla stared at her for a long moment. What did she mean? Confidence? Only one person? Was there someone here who had manipulated so well that the matter was a *fait accompli*? In that case, who? Martin Bernheim? He lived nearby, only a couple of miles away, and he could drop in whenever it suited him. That was a clear advantage over those who lived in Stockholm and at most could only write or afford an occasional phone call. And right now Martin was sitting beside her, so he must be the one Aunt Charlotte had confidence in. Somewhere in the back of her mind Ulla reminded herself that she had given him seven points when she was figuring out the odds. Oh, well. In any case, she was painfully aware that Aunt Charlotte had never shown any great signs of confidence when it came to her or Fredrik. Unless you could take it as confidence when she revealed that she knew Fredrik called her a hag.

Oh, no! Suddenly she understood who it must be. But before she could formulate the thought Miss Lethander went on. "He hasn't arrived yet, but I know he's coming, since he promised he would. He has a lot of important things to talk over with me. I mean Mauritz, of course. I have always had greater confidence in Mauritz than in the rest of you when it comes to managing my properties and giving me advice. Mauritz is a first-rate businessman. He is accustomed to handling such things."

Thank god, thought Ulla. It's Mauritz. And the reason is not like or dislike, but business. She should have realized right away that it couldn't be the Bernheims, since that side of the family had no sense at all in business matters. Martin—it was a miracle he hadn't ruined himself with his horses. And Victor, the talk of the family, with his sports cars and his women. Mauritz was naturally the most appropriate one. Still —she felt an upsurge of apprehension again—if Mauritz is involved in managing Aunt Charlotte's estate, they would have to ask what the disadvantage to them would be. It was, of course, an advantage for Mauritz. Now, why hadn't her branch of the family been brought in? Fredrik wasn't stupid. If for no other reason Aunt Charlotte should recognize that, since she knew that he was thinking of setting up his own workshop—and at *his* age. They could have consulted Carl, even if he is a little young for such things. He doesn't lack talent and he understands money matters—you could even say that he is a penny pincher. Wasn't he the obvious choice as treasurer for his Socialist-labor group?

"This does not mean, naturally, that anyone's rights are to be trampled underfoot. No matter what you say about me, I am fair and all of you at this table have claims on me. More than anyone else, and certainly more than the public inheritance fund. I have not been granted the pleasure—and perhaps have been spared the disappointments—of a husband and children. God knows whether I would have wanted it . . ." She paused, in thought for a long while before continuing in a low voice, almost to herself. "Well, there are rights and rights. Rights as heirs, of course. But the important thing is how I shall divide things up in my will. I am now informing you that I have made a will, and you are all in it—with a certain exception—not only the heads of families but also your children."

Ulla closed her eyes. If the children inherited equally, her branch of the family would do as well as the Bernheims and better than Mauritz. The exception—who could that be? It must be Malin. They all knew that she had married that foreigner not only against Mauritz's wishes but also against Aunt Charlotte's. Ulla raised her eyes and examined the Yugoslav. He was sitting quietly, with his head bowed, almost as if asleep. That was not so remarkable, perhaps, since he didn't know a word of Swedish. But he must understand the general significance of what was going on. He could hardly help but know that old Aunt Charlotte was pulling the strings attached to her nieces and nephews. You could pick that up from the air. One point credit in the seating plan, she thought with satisfaction. But before the thought came to a conclusion, the headache that had been threatening made itself known with a shooting pain from temple to temple.

Aunt Charlotte continued. "I have made one or two exceptions. One is Ulla, who will receive a little more than the rest of you. She shall also get Lucy, if Lucy is still alive." She stroked the cat's back gently. "The other is little Charlene. It would not be fair to go so far down into the youngest generation without taking into consideration all the children that may be born into other branches of the family. I have therefore stopped at my brother's grandchildren—with the single exception of Malin."

Ulla felt the shooting pain again. The unpleasant announcement that she was to get the damned cat was outweighed only by the other announcement, that Charlene could count on nothing. She let her gaze slide from the black-haired foreigner over to John, who was sitting diagonally across the table from her. She liked John. She tried to see how he was reacting. Actually, she would have liked to see how young Charlotte was reacting, but Carl was sitting between her and Charlotte and she did not want to attract attention by leaning forward. John looked completely unconcerned. She suddenly remembered that he had laughed a little contemptuously when she, Ulla, had suggested that the baby should be christened Charlene. Charlotte was not satisfactory, since it would have led to confusion between mother and daughter, but Charlene was both sweet and suitable.

"Suitable?" John had said. "Suitable for what?"

Ulla had been unable to answer, for she was not so stupid as to miss the sarcasm. Nor did Fredrik make things any better when he said something like, "The hag is so old that she won't even notice what we call the kid. Anyway, this is a good time to say to hell with her."

Ulla answered with tears in her eyes, for she really liked Aunt Charlotte, "Do you really mean that?" And Fredrik answered, "No . . ."

"It is true that I don't understand young people very well these days," the old lady went on. "There are so many new things today. No one can demand that I keep up with them all. But may I just emphasize that the apportioning of my estate will be somewhat influenced by the fact that one or two of you have views far too extreme for me to approve or accept. If you don't believe in private property, you can hardly claim it for yourself. And I'm not one to disturb anyone's convictions by leading him into temptation . . ."

Ulla could feel herself going pale. Aunt Lethander must have meant Carl, and with great discomfort she realized the old lady clearly did not share her own opinion either of Carl's good sense and judgment or of his financial abilities. She should have known that that horrid little Socialist badge adorning his jacket would have unpleasant consequences for him as well as for other people. It represented an utter lack of respect for life as it was—both for human beings and possessions. Trouble, destruction, and subversion. Well, he would have an opportunity now of seeing how that badge had destroyed his own chances, although it would have been easy to compromise slightly. He might even have increased his chances; for anyone making an effort to gain the favor of old Aunt Lethander, an extra zero on the end of a goodly sum would not be beyond the bounds of possibility . . .

"On the other hand, I think it is important to try to convert a misled person to a more positive view of life. And perhaps . . . perhaps that can be done by exceptional generosity toward the person whose mind one wishes to open."

The word "generosity" slipped as mild as milk into Ulla's ears and ignited a fresh spark in her eyes. The darling old thing—how wise she was after all. And how right of her to try to achieve with the help of her money the conversion that Ulla's sighs and Fredrik's oaths had failed to effect. What Aunt Lethander had just said was as good as a promise that Carl could reckon on *more* than what was due him—a prize for his idealism, a reward for the righteous struggle for ideological movements that were all part of a progressive, active youth . . .

"As her father has also succeeded so well in many difficult business assignments and increased my capital, neither is that entirely unfair. In addition, there is only *one* child in that branch of the family."

Ulla stiffened. She means *Malin*, she thought. Not Carl. So Malin was also one of those people with no respect for society and secure development. That was news to Ulla. She let her gaze slide across the table until it fell on Mauritz's young daughter, clearly sitting far too close to Aunt Lethander. Oh, yes. There was a certain impertinence, even ruthlessness, around her mouth, which was also shaping into an inward smile at the old lady's words. Greedily inward. What would she use the money for? Donate it to the revolution? Throw it into the streets? Melt it down and pour the molten metal down the throats of capitalist enemies, as Carl used to say when in a joking mood. Supposing Malin were like that? It was understandable that young men, full of *joie de vivre*, liked to use their surplus energy on politics. Yes, one could understand that, maybe even respect it. But women—never.

The old lady had fallen silent. She was looking around with friendly eyes, the silence so intense that a leaf would have been heard falling onto the thick, pale blue dining-room carpet.

But she soon started to speak again, her voice more brittle

than ever. "My time will soon be up. My greatest wish and the last of any importance to me is that all of you sitting around this table—Mauritz, too, of course—will love each other, because you are all part of the same family. I'd like to sing just as Victor did a little while ago—love, love, love . . . And now I've helped you on the way by bringing you all together for my birthday. It's been a great pleasure to me that you've all responded to my summons—kindly and un-selfishly."

There was another pause. Ulla heard feet shifting against chair legs and noticed the exchange of glances. She was hor-rified to hear tittering from the end of the table, but then was soon calm again, not to say satisfied, when she realized it was one of the Bernheims misbehaving. Veronica was looking with great interest at the foreigner beside her, which was hardly appropriate, considering he and Malin had been mar-ried only a month or two. Ulla also had a vague feeling that a southerner like him would not need much encouragement to forget what one should and should not do in a Swedish marriage . . .

"Take this opportunity to talk to each other," said Aunt Charlotte emphatically. "That's probably not so difficult for you young people, as young people can always agree. But you older people, disliking each other for no reason at all, you must get to know each other better and strengthen your common bond, because you have the same blood in your veins and because you bear the responsibility for the family. That's my greatest wish—that you respect and love each other. I thought you might find it difficult to take the first step, so I invited you all here. When I wrote that anyone who didn't want to come would lose a great deal, that was only to make the decision easier for you. I meant the experience of family fellowship and exchange of ideas, of course."

Ulla drooped. God, had she been guarding against only *that* risk, bouncing about in a bus for nine frightful hours. And taking several days off from work. Well, that didn't matter all that much to Fredrik. He could easily get away, as he had a responsible job. But John. And Carl, who had his lectures. She was feeling uneasy again, and the unpleasant headache was creeping back between her temples. Family fellowship and exchange of ideas! The only fellowship she knew in the people around the table was—rivalry, distrust, and fear of being forgotten the moment the old woman died. Supposing she had sensed that that moment was near? Perhaps she *knew?* All that photographing. Poor, dear old thing, was she going to tell them—*now?* That would be terrible. It would be much more fun if it happened without warning, as a surprise—"Have you heard that the old girl's dead?" That was the way such information should come. If you knew about it beforehand, you would just have a guilty conscience and you would have to try to do a whole lot of rather unnecessary things. No, thought Ulla, one shouldn't know about it beforehand. That would be like preparing for a party before you got the invitation. She looked intently at the old lady to see if the thin, wrinkled face revealed anything. But she saw nothing but friendly resolution, and to crown everything, Aunt Lethander unexpectedly raised her hand and waved benignly at them.

"Tonight we'll have a party," she said. "Tonight you can celebrate my birthday and kick up your heels. I'll probably join in for a while, if you promise me that I won't kill the fun."

Then she bent over, picked up her cat, swung around, and went out through the pantry door. Most of them sitting there watching saw her go down the hallway, into her little private apartment at the end of the passage, and close the door behind her. Quietly and unobtrusively.

2

VERONICA

I HADN'T BEEN TO THE OLD HOUSE FOR YEARS, NOT SINCE I was preparing for my confirmation and was staying with Great-aunt Lethander, because she wanted me to be confirmed by the local minister. That was ten years ago, the last summer Vera lived at home. That autumn she moved to Stockholm, where she first got an office job. Then she took her university entrance exam in her spare time and started reading the usual old things—sociology, psychology, and political science. In contrast to most students, she took her work seriously and got very high grades. As the grades kept coming in, and she became involved in political societies of the more radical kind, she cut her hair shorter and shorter, wore glasses with thinner and thinner frames and bigger and bigger lenses, and her contempt for the Establishment grew. For a year or two she tried to push me in the same direction, but with little success. Despite our differences we shared a little three-room apartment in Engelbrecht Street, a comfortable distance from my own boutique on Svea Road and from Humlegård Park, Vera's usual starting point for demonstrations.

We were also now sharing a room at Aunt Lethander's. There were two ocher-yellow painted wings to Aunt Lethander's house, each one containing an apartment with combined bedroom and living room, a small hall, a kitchenette, and a bathroom. There was also one large single room with its own entrance in the gable end facing away from the main house. Those single rooms were usually used only on occasions when everywhere else was occupied.

So Vera and I shared an apartment in the east wing. Malin and her Yugoslav were in the west wing. On the other side of the wall from us, in the large single room, Ellen was staying the night, as she had not planned to remain more than one night—because of her farm animals. Then it was easy to work out that Mauritz, Malin's father, would take over the corresponding large room in the other wing when he arrived.

I was feeling uneasy after lunch, which was not all that surprising, as the taunts and hostility among the families had been so blatant. Mostly among the older people, of course. They were the ones sitting on the branch nearest to the prey, like vultures, I thought, waiting for time to give them a rich feast.

I drew back the flowered curtains to open the window. It was terribly close inside, and someone had said that we could expect a thunderstorm before the evening.

I saw Aunt Lethander outside. She was on her way down the broad front steps with the housekeeper, Alma. I knew at once what they were doing. She was taking her midday walk. Every day at this time, just after lunch, the old ladies used to take a walk in the forest. It had always been the same. In sunshine and rain. Summer and winter. I watched them crossing the gravel and saw them nodding to the Yugoslav, who was bare to the waist and sunning himself outside the other guest wing. He leaped to his feet and bowed almost exaggeratedly politely, I thought, but on the other hand it showed that he'd been well brought up and I was sure Aunt Lethander appreciated the gesture. I'd had Sergej Rosceff as my partner at the table, which wasn't all that much fun, as he knew no Swedish, and not even English. Almost in desperation, I tried flirting a little with him, but he didn't seem to understand that, either.

With her arm under Alma's, Aunt Lethander turned through the wide iron gates in the spirea hedge. They followed the driveway, walking in the middle of the road, the stone walls running along both sides like mossy bulwarks, and then finally they vanished around a bend in the forest road down toward the sea. One of them was a slight, small blue shadow, the other a stout, waddling guard beside her.

Just as I was about to leave the window someone else came down the steps. It was Charles. He had put on his jogging suit and running shoes, and without looking to the right or the left, or showing any sign of having seen either me or the Yugoslav, he jogged away in the same direction as the two old ladies, running softly and smoothly, his curly hair flapping and bouncing in time with his steps. I had met Charles a few times in Stockholm, the last time a couple of months back. My sister, Vera, and Carl belonged to the same political society, and after an anti-U.S.A. demonstration—or whatever it was—she had invited him back for chicken and red wine. So that I wouldn't feel too isolated by their anticapitalist discussions, Vera had phoned Charles and invited him, too, and as he had just married and was still totally absorbed in the girl, Gittan, naturally she came, too. Just as well, because otherwise it would have been nothing but a meeting of cousins. When Gittan heard that I had a boutique, she got excited and wanted to come and look, and try things on. She came a few days later. While she was at it, Victor appeared. He used to drop in occasionally "on a hunt," as he called it, and my boutique was a dependable source of game. Victor always had his camera with him. If he then met a pretty girl, he would persuade her to pose for a few photographs, and if they turned out well, he sometimes sold them to one of those magazines that have centerfolds.

Victor was bewitched by Gittan, unable to take his eyes off her, and when she left, he went with her. She became a photograph, too. In one of those magazines. He came in and showed it to me sometime later, full of enthusiasm.

"What a girl," he said. "Look at her hair—long, billowing,

and golden blond—and her arms, like slim serpents. Don't you think she's fantastic? And under that sweater—Jesus, what a body. Like a deer when she moves . . . ahhhh."

He collapsed into a low-slung canvas chair. I felt a slight sting of envy, for even though he was my brother, he might well have occasionally said he thought I wasn't bad-looking, either.

"I can't see her moving," I said. "Anyhow, I've heard through the grapevine that she's pretty dumb, poor thing."

That went right over Victor's head. He just sat there in the chair looking dopey, staring at the centerfold he was holding in his hand.

I didn't know whether they had been meeting since the photo session, but during lunch at Aunt Lethander's I realized Charles was raging with jealousy, even if he was hiding it well. I suddenly knew that the meeting of Victor and Charles and Gittan might cause some trouble. Victor could be really nervy when he wanted to. It hadn't surprised me in the least when he had kissed Gittan at the table, and it wasn't entirely out of the question that he had done it just to annoy Charles. He didn't care at all whether there was a scandal. I could also imagine that he would continue his pursuit of Gittan if she gave him the slightest encouragement. And I felt very strongly that this was exactly what she was doing.

Despite the heat billowing in through the window, I felt cold all over. It was just as oppressive as it had been inside before I'd opened the window, so I put on a pair of sandals and decided to find Vera. She must be somewhere in the big house.

The hall was deserted and silent, but as cool and beautiful as a church, with its lovely polished parquet floor glimmering in the meager light from the two high, narrow draped windows on either side of the front door. Straight ahead was a magnificent staircase up to the first floor, where we had had lunch. I've always thought it almost like a symbol of the wide road to splendor and kingly fortunes, the banisters at attention up the sides with their turned oak posts, and high up above a glimpse of the chandelier, which when switched on made the whole hall glitter and the wall panels shine like mother-of-pearl between the well-stocked bookcases with their sweet-smelling leather bindings. I didn't go up, but turned left and went along the long corridor that ran down to the kitchen. About halfway down was the foot of another staircase, narrow and quite steep, leading up to the corresponding corridor on the first floor, linking the dining room with Aunt Lethander's separate apartment, workroom, sewing room, and bedroom.

I had hardly taken two steps beyond those stairs when I heard someone coming heavily downstairs behind me. I turned around, almost frightened by the sudden panting noise that broke the silence.

It was Fredrik, my uncle by marriage, his shirt unbuttoned almost down to his trousers, his tie still around his neck, undone at the collar. At first he put his finger to his lips, as if realizing he had frightened me and wanting to stop me from crying out. Then he beckoned to me with one hand while he scratched at the coarse mat of hair on his chest with the other.

"Say," he whispered, "do you know where the old girl keeps her liquor? It was hell having nothing to drink with lunch. She must keep some liquor somewhere."

He winked at me confidentially. I'd never really liked Fredrik much, but now I felt a distinct distaste. I stared at him as ironically as I could. His small eyes were pinkish and sunk in two wrinkled bags down on his cheeks, where stubble was already appearing again, although he had looked freshly shaved at lunch. At first I thought I'd say I had no idea where Aunt Lethander kept her supply of liquor, or whether she had any at all, but then I changed my mind. I saw that a struggle between hope and fear was raging inside him, so I spoke dryly and half whispering, just as he had.

"She used to in the old days," I said. "And since you don't come to see her all that often, she's sure to have some left."

"Where?"

Before I had time to answer, the kitchen door opened and Victor came out, and when he saw us he laughed nastily. He had changed into a bright red shirt and black jeans, and was holding a glass of something brown in his hand.

"What a nose you have," he said to Fredrik. "You're after the whiskey, of course. It's in the kitchen, in the cupboard on the right, on the top shelf by the ventilator."

He winked and took a small sip. I tried to look disapproving, but actually felt like laughing, and when he winked at me, too, I turned away and giggled. Fredrik was looking around as if anxious not to be discovered. Then he stared at Victor and said with great solemnity, "Much obliged." But he didn't go into the kitchen. Instead he swung his considerable bulk around and vanished back up the stairs.

Victor grinned so broadly that his eyes vanished into glittering narrow slits. Then, gesturing toward the glass, he said, "It's not for me, darling. It's for Martin. And sure as hell he's going to need it. Big brother Victor's going to squeeze some cash out of the old man, and if you like, you can come and learn how to do it."

So I went up with him to Martin's room. None of us children, neither Vera, Victor, nor myself, had ever called our father anything but Martin. He wanted it that way, which also meant none of us ever called our mother anything but Ellen. "Martin's room" was Aunt Lethander's name for one of the two large bedrooms on the top floor, which were always made up and ready for casual overnight guests. The rooms were next to each other, both with doors out onto the top landing—where the bookcases and the chandeliers were— and in both doors the narrow topmost panel had been replaced by a pane of glass. Originally, a long time ago, Aunt Lethander's father had used one of these rooms as his bedroom. Right in the middle of the room was a beautiful open stove with a large hearth and a cone-shaped white flue that ran through the ceiling into the chimney.

The other room had been used by Aunt Lethander's mother. It had no open fireplace, and in the middle of the room there was a low, circular white table surrounded by comfortable, small low armchairs. The whole room was decorated in white and rose—a wide white bed, rose-colored wallpaper from long before the turn of the century, white curtains, and rose mats. After Aunt Lethander's parents had died, both rooms had remained empty until Martin Bernheim had come to the house for the first time after he had married Ellen. Then one of the rooms had become "Martin's room," but the other had not become Ellen's—eventually it became Victor's.

Victor lightly drummed on the door with the tips of his fingers. Without waiting for a reply, he opened the door and walked in. I followed him, but halted rather guardedly on the threshold. Martin was sitting reading by the window. When we went into the room, he put down his paper and got up out of the armchair. Victor walked straight up to him, holding out the glass of whiskey. Martin looked bewildered but took the glass, sniffed it quickly, then put it down on the windowsill without tasting it. Victor looked at him.

"Have a drink," he said.

Martin laughed, then, making an abrupt gesture with his large sunburned hand, the veins in it like coarse ropes, he stopped laughing as abruptly as he had started.

"No, thanks. I've got to drive in a little while."

"Where are you going?"

"Home. Ellen has to get back to tend the hens."

"And tonight?"

"Of course we'll be at the party. Then we'll stay the night. What did you bring that whiskey for?"

Victor smiled mysteriously and started wandering around the room, Martin watching him. I suddenly sensed an unpleasant tension beginning to grow between them. Martin and Victor were terribly alike. When Victor reached his fifties, he would probably look exactly as Martin did now. His dark brown hair would probably be silvery gray like Martin's —yes, it was gray, but a vital gray—and the coming quarter of a century would probably sculpt his face just as ruggedly square. Martin was wearing the pale lilac shirt with two pockets and ornamental buttons I had given him for Christmas. It had come from the boutique, and although the designer had probably had a jet-set young man in mind, it suited Martin perfectly.

As Victor kept circling, Martin's frown deepened. Suddenly he said, "You're up to some damn monkey business. Out with it."

Victor stopped and looked straight at him. "You've got to give me some money."

"What the hell did you say? I'm supposed to give you money? Why should I give you any money?"

"Because I need it."

Victor had lowered his voice, and I thought he sounded horribly cold and hard as he spoke. I was both curious and profoundly disturbed by his asking me to accompany him. I tried to think of a way to intervene in some way to lighten the atmosphere, but I didn't know how. Make a joke of it, perhaps? But it wasn't easy to think up anything amusing at that moment. Perhaps I ought to leave? But if this was going to develop into a quarrel, then perhaps it would be just as well if I stayed to try to smooth things over.

"I've got to have the money," Victor went on, then added almost in despair, "Why the hell can't you understand that I wouldn't for one moment ask you for money if I could avoid it."

Martin looked coldly at him. Then his lip curled and he snorted, "Got to. Even if you had a fortune, it wouldn't last you longer than the length of your nose, what with your cars. And women. I'm not going to interfere with your way of life, but I'm not going to help you finance it. Have that whiskey yourself. You seem to need some calming down."

I couldn't keep quiet any longer.

"Come on," I said to Victor. "Let's go."

"No, wait," said Victor. "Because this is it, damn it."

He leaned forward slowly, not taking his eyes off Martin for one moment. Then he slid his hand into his back pocket and pulled out a piece of paper. He unfolded it, slowly and ceremoniously, then handed it to Martin, who took it with such a heavy frown that his eyebrows met above his nose. Martin held the paper away from him in that typical way that showed he really needed glasses. (He used to say that there was no point in his getting glasses, since he would probably lose them in the stables the very first day.) As he read, the lines around his mouth and the expression in his eyes hardened. When he had finished, he folded the paper and gave it back to Victor.

The seed of something dangerous lay in that piece of paper. I realized that. I'd followed the scene between them with a feeling that a catastrophe was about to occur.

For a few moments Martin was quiet, and then he said sharply, "You don't have to pay that. No court in the world would make you pay, so tear it up into small pieces and forget the whole thing."

"You don't know my friends."

"No, thank god."

"This is a matter of honor."

"No honor is worth fifteen thousand."

"Hell, don't you see that they'll mutilate me, cut me up? I have to pay them."

Martin looked unmoved.

"I'd like to know how you got yourself into such a mess. And then had the nerve to come ask me for money."

Victor exuded the venom of a cobra. "Haven't *you* ever gambled? What's the difference between poker and horses? Damn it, you embezzled my entire inheritance for your horses before I even got a chance to do anything about it . . ."

Martin smiled coldly. "You mean, increased its value."

"Your damned stables aren't worth a rotten egg."

"Come now—they're worth something as dog food, anyhow."

Victor drew a deep breath, then moved swiftly to the window, snatched up the glass, and emptied it in one gulp. When he turned back to Martin again, his lips were glistening from the liquor and he kept striking the palm of his hand with the empty glass.

"You must pay this debt."

Martin shrugged. "Not me. If you want to pay it, that's your business. You can hit up Aunt Lethander. She's got the money, but I don't think you'll get much sympathy."

"Don't you have any?"

"No."

"All right."

There was another silence. Victor went over to the fireplace and put the glass down with a bang on the whitewashed frieze. His face was flushed under his sunburn, making him look almost brown in the shadow of the room. His dark hair flapped on his forehead as he nodded his head back and forth, as if trying to demonstrate how hopeless he thought Martin was.

I sensed the second act in this drama was just about to open, and then he suddenly said shrilly, "How much is *your* honor worth? How much, Martin?"

Martin looked at him in surprise.

"I don't see . . ."

"If you want me to set a price, then it's exactly fifteen thousand, Martin. I have a piece of paper. I've had a small piece of paper since the last time I was at home. Do you know which piece of paper?"

He looked challengingly at Martin, who was standing perfectly still by the window, his arms hanging down, his mouth half open, uncertainty in his questioning gray eyes.

"A letter that was tucked away in that desk drawer you've always been so secretive about. There was something else there, too, that I'm sure you shouldn't have."

Martin had pulled himself together at last. "You found a letter?"

Victor nodded, then jerked his head toward the fireplace. "You can have it back for fifteen thousand. That'll give you a chance to burn it. You can have it today if you like. Now—this minute. For fifteen thousand. This letter, you see, I've saved as a little insurance policy, and I know for damn sure what it's worth to you."

"A letter . . ."

Martin looked at me with an unspoken question in his eyes. I realized what he meant and slowly shook my head, nauseated by Victor's loathsome blackmail attempt. I hoped Martin would do something, go up to him and hit him perhaps, or burst out laughing, or tell him to go to hell—anything. But he did none of those. He just stood there, utterly helpless and exhausted.

"Does Ellen know?" said Victor.

Martin shook his head. "Ellen doesn't rummage in my drawers."

"Stella, Stella, Stella," said Victor suddenly in a low, chattering voice, leaning toward Martin as if he wanted the words to penetrate his head.

Then he paused before going on. "You'd better realize that I know what it's all about."

Martin sank into the armchair, staring vacantly ahead of him. Then he noticed that the newspaper had fallen to the floor and he picked it up and slowly started folding it, apparently playing for time.

"You can look on it as a loan if you like," said Victor. "An advance. Fifteen thousand. And if it's any consolation to you, you should know that they're not kids that've got their claws in me, either."

Martin looked wearily at him.

"Where's the letter?"

"Oh, no. We'll talk about that later. And don't think this is pleasant for me. How do you want to do it?"

"I'll call you first. There's a lot of bluffing in poker."

"Go ahead. You check. But you can't check the camera."

"No."

Martin looked at his son, uncertainly and furtively, for a long time.

"Has anyone read it?" he said, then stopped. "Oh, well, it doesn't matter. Stella's gone."

"Of course, Stella's gone."

I caught a strange undertone in Victor's echo and saw clearly that he now had the advantage over Martin. But I didn't understand anything. Stella. I remembered Stella very well, although it had been many years since I'd had any reason to think about her. I'd never really had any reason to before, actually, except once. That was late one evening, when Vera and I had gone to bed, and I was just about to fall asleep. I was woken up from my half sleep by Vera crying, weeping and thumping her clenched fists against the bedstead and half whispering into her pillow, "I *hate* him. And I hate Stella, hate her, hate, hate . . ." I sat up in bed and almost started crying, too. Then I switched on the lamp and Vera sat up, her eyes swollen and red, and I asked her what it was all about.

She wouldn't tell me—she never did—so I'd forgotten all about it until this moment. But now I had some idea. There must have been something between Martin and Stella. So Martin had a letter from her in his desk drawer—stupid Martin—and Victor had taken the letter. There was just one thing that seemed odd: Why did that letter mean so much to Martin that Victor now had the upper hand? I looked at Martin in surprise.

Slowly he got out of the chair and took two deep breaths. Then he went across to the door and held it open as he stared intently and without wavering at Victor. "You can go now. You can both go. That fifteen thousand. I'll think about it until tomorrow. We can't do business this evening because of the old girl's birthday party. I'll let you know tomorrow."

As we went down the wide staircase to the lower hall I knew that Victor had won the match against his father. I also knew that he knew it, too, because he was laughing quietly with satisfaction and almost dancing down the stairs. What I did not know was how Martin would get his hands on that money, or whether Victor really needed it to pay some gambling debt, or whether he was truly as hard pressed as he'd made out. And what I definitely didn't know, didn't guess, and couldn't have foreseen was that Martin would not let Victor know the next day, nor would an answer be given to Victor, because by morning, both Martin and Victor would be dead.

3

ELLEN

THE HEN HOUSE WAS A LONG, LOW WOODEN BUILDING, PAINTED red, forming a wing of the stables, in which Martin Bernheim had a string of about twenty thoroughbred horses with pedigrees that gave him hope that one of them, one fine day, would lay the foundation for another fortune in prizes and wins on the racetracks of the nation.

Ellen was sensibly skeptical about the whole thing. Over the years, she had watched her husband's family inheritance, which had been considerable and included acres of good woodland with standing timber, being used up for one pea-brained investment after another, such as the purchase of doubtful sites in Florida (no doubt on some swamp or other); or venture capital for optimistic inventors; or on a so-called education for Victor, who considered investment in contacts more profitable than college fees. More money was squandered on Vera, who had become an enthusiast for feminist causes and considered it her duty to help finance both the women's movement and left-wing marches and demonstrations. And on Veronica, the lovely Veronica, who had romantically staked all on reviving the eighteenth century in her little boutique on Svea Road in Stockholm.

Ellen had long since become resigned to this. She realized that the mortgaged timberland could not possibly be felled at the rate demanded by current interest rates. She also realized that the local government would never find the sum of money Martin was demanding for it to use the land for building a residential and shopping center project. Martin's suggested price per square meter had alone produced in the eyes of the officials a glint of compulsory sale by eminent domain.

In other words, Ellen had not only witnessed Martin's family fortune rapidly disappearing over the years, but she had also realized that nothing short of a miracle would bring their finances back to a good condition again. Aunt Lethander, or rather her demise, was to be that miracle. But as time had gone by, wearing out everyone except Aunt Lethander, Ellen had become resigned, ironically, maybe even slightly cynically. When—several years ago—the horses had started appearing at the manor in gaily painted horse trailers, she had started her own business: a chicken farm. She ran it purposefully and almost lovingly along old-fashioned lines, with straw in the nest boxes, a hen yard outside, and a virile cock which she changed a few times a year, since he had to service several hundred hens. The only concession she made to modern technology was the electrically driven, thermostatically controlled hatchery, into which she regularly fed about a thousand eggs. The day-old chickens were delivered to a large breeder in Västergötland. The rest of the eggs were sent daily by bus to Svensson's grocery store in Gislaved.

Ellen bent down to check the temperature on the thermostat before going on to the nesting boxes to fill the basket on her arm with newly laid eggs. When she got home she changed into her faded old overalls, now as soft as velvet after the years of washing. Naturally, Aunt Lethander had to have some eggs. She had already been given a basketful when they had gone over for lunch. But when Ellen had found out how many people were staying for the weekend, she was ashamed she had not taken more with her. Just one basket might seem stingy, and, after all, Aunt Lethander was going to be *ninety*.

Ellen let her thoughts hover around old Aunt Lethander. Perhaps her renewed offering of eggs would turn out to be a good investment, which one day would show a greater return than she might imagine, for she was really the only person who showed that kind of everyday consideration for Aunt Lethander.

She knew some people were more interested in the old lady's money than the old lady herself, and other kinds of investments were made from many directions to secure returns. The Svenssons, for instance. They never risked material goods, of course. That would be against Ulla's nature. But Christmas cards. Regularly. Flattering letters. Then that cunning idea of having the children baptized after Aunt Lethander; whether a girl or a boy, each child was to carry on the name. First names: Charlotte, Charles, Carl. Ellen smiled ironically as she groped around in the nest until she found an egg that was still warm.

Then there was Mauritz. His mother had been Aunt Lethander's most loved and spoiled niece. All indications were that that love had been transferred to the son, at least until the day Mauritz had married Stella. Ellen remembered very well how deeply disturbed and annoyed the old lady had been when she heard that Mauritz, in great secrecy and much too precipitately, in her opinion, had married an actress. But she also remembered Aunt Lethander being very upset when Stella had died at only thirty-six, and what was even more devastating was that it had happened during a visit to the old lady. Ellen had done all she could at the time to console Mauritz, but he was not really the kind of person who needed consolation.

Mauritz was so incredibly rational, even when it came to emotions. Cold, many people would say, but Ellen was not sure that was the right adjective. She would have said prudent. Yes, just prudent. He was sufficiently intelligent to be prudent.

She smiled inwardly. Mauritz's name had not been mentioned in the Bernheim home for years. There was a chilly chasm between Martin and Mauritz, and although she knew nothing about it, she had always had a feeling it had something to do with Stella.

Martin had been interested in Stella. Ellen had never dared let on that she knew, because had she done so, Martin would have been furious. That was Martin's usual reaction when he wanted to hide something, and the more he raged, the more he usually had to hide. Like that time, for instance, when he had been cheated by a horse dealer and bought Prince of the Sea on the name alone and without bothering to look in the stud books. A more thorough investigation would have immediately shown that the Prince's forebears, hence chances for profitability, were no better than those of any other old sea horse. Martin had tried to hide that fiasco from her. And there was also the time he had sold the oak wood down by the lake to Göranson's timber firm for a song. Göranson had come out one Sunday morning with a bulging wallet, a bottle of fine old Scotch, and the knowledge that Martin was in dire need of cash. He had asked Martin whether he had any idea of the worth of the oak wood down by the lake.

"No," said Martin. "I've never had it valued. But there must be a couple of hundred trees there."

"And what do you think a standing tree is worth, then?" said Göranson.

"Well, you can get a couple of hundred, I would think."

"I'll give you three," said Göranson, taking out his wallet. He counted thirty thousand-kronor notes onto the table in front of Martin.

"Is it a deal?" he asked.

To be fair, Ellen thought she remembered Martin hesitating.

"If you agree, we can sign here and now," said Göranson, pulling out a document containing everything except Martin's name. Göranson pushed the paper toward him, took a silver Parker pen from his inside pocket, and placed it beside the contract.

"You've got a minute to think it over," he said. "If you're not interested, I'm going up to Johansnäs to buy from Malmgren. It'll be more expensive, but there are a few more oaks there."

Martin laughed.

"Okay," he said. "You can have mine, but I want the rest of what you've got in your wallet, too."

Ellen remembered closing her eyes and thinking, There goes Martin being cheated again. Göranson had also laughed. Once, then again, then a burst of laughter, which infected Martin, who also started laughing. As they sat there laughing helplessly, Göranson pulled out his wallet again and took out seven hundred-kronor notes, a few tens, and a five. Finally he got his change purse out of his trouser pocket and emptied it onto the table. Martin doubled up with laughter and signed. A few days later, Martin heard that Göranson had sold the oak wood to a lumber dealer in Halmstad for nearly five hundred thousand kronor. Standing trees. But this time the wood had been valued. Martin had tried to hide the end of the story from her. Ellen had allowed the oak wood and Prince and other stupidities Martin had left himself in for to sink into oblivion. She could have been bitter about it, but she was not. On the other hand, she sometimes found her feelings for Martin had turned into indifference, although a somewhat committed indifference. She knew he needed her and she didn't really mind that he didn't realize it. She was there when he wanted her, and she also intuitively sensed when the need was there.

During the ride back from Aunt Lethander's, she knew something had happened—something had upset Martin. She did not know what and he said nothing. She wondered whether it had anything to do with Mauritz, whether he was disappointed Mauritz had not been there, since he had almost certainly prepared himself for the meeting. It had been years since they had last met. That was when Mauritz and Stella used to come out regularly and stay for summer vacations with them at the manor.

Ellen groped absentmindedly in the next nest, not noticing that it was occupied by a hen, which rushed out, squawking in fright, and half ran, half flew for the opening to the yard. *She* had been worried about the meeting with Mauritz, not on her own behalf but on Martin's. Mauritz was prudent, true, but he was also as hard as flint, sly, cold, and ruthless. Martin was spontaneous and hot-tempered, given as much to a hearty laugh as to spluttering rage. It wouldn't take all that much provocation on Mauritz's part for Martin to lose his temper, and Ellen knew his right arm could strike like a sledgehammer.

There were two eggs in the last nest, and they just filled the basket. She walked to the doorway, which shone like a white rectangle against the sunny yard outside, hooked the door shut behind her, and walked toward the house. It was a lovely two-story house, painted gray, with curved mossy red roof tiles, shaded by tall maples on either side of the front-door veranda. As she walked toward the back door she passed Martin's study, on the ground floor. The windows were low enough for her to look right in, and one of the windows was open.

She saw Martin inside. He was standing in front of his desk, his back to her, talking on the phone. A drawer was pulled out. Suddenly his hand fell, and for a few moments he stood motionless without replacing the receiver, then clutched violently at his head with his other hand. Before replacing the receiver, he slammed the drawer with a bang and locked it. Then he pulled out another drawer and took out something she could not see. She stood there, not moving, watching him, at the same time knowing he would not like her witnessing this scene, and grateful for the shadow of the maples and the neutral color of her overalls.

Suddenly he turned around to face the window and she

flushed when she saw what he had in his hand. He was play-ing with it, hefting it, and finally he slipped it into the inner pocket of his jacket. She closed her eyes and swallowed. When she looked up again, she met his gaze through the window. He crossed the room swiftly and, leaning on the sill, said, "Oh, so you got another basketful after all. Good." He looked searchingly at her, and she realized he already knew she had been spying on him. He grinned broadly, his face alight.

"Vera just phoned," he said. "I told her you were in the hen house."

The smile vanished when she did not answer right away, and she had the impression he was suddenly studying her, suspiciously and searchingly, almost anxiously. She picked up an egg and held it out to him.

"They're getting bigger and bigger," she said. "It must be the maize. Maize is money in the pocket for hens. Even though you said . . ." She didn't finish the thought but con-tented herself with a sigh and put the egg back in the basket.

He laughed again.

"Sure. You can bet they're golden eggs you're producing. You can bet you'll get the old hen to lay money with those eggs just as well as you get those hens to lay eggs with maize."

"What did Vera want?"

He looked ironically at her. "Since I was the one who hap-pened to pick up the phone, she didn't want anything. She wanted to talk to you."

"And . . ."

"And when I said you were out in the hen house, she said it wasn't that important and it could wait until tonight." He glanced at his watch. "I don't really feel like going tonight," he went on. "The whole thing's unpleasant. But I suppose we can't really get out of it."

"We have to put up with it," said Ellen. "I'm taking things as they come."

"Those damned Svenssons make me boil. They'll do ab-solutely anything to . . ."

He screwed up his eyes, which were clear and vital and almost the same color as the hair tumbling over his broad, sunburned forehead. The corners of his mouth turned up in a quirky smile.

"But that's life—you can't help stepping on everyone else's toes when you're all dancing around the golden calf. Well, I'm not worried. We can handle the steps all right."

"I hope so," she said, then paused. "Mauritz, too."

"Sure. Mauritz, too."

Although she had listened for the slightest worrying shift of tone in his voice, she could detect nothing. He was still smiling. Then she went on, because she was determined to get some reaction.

"You haven't been in contact with Mauritz since Stella died, have you?"

"No."

"Sometimes I've wondered why things have been so quiet."

"What d'you mean, quiet?"

She met his eyes and the glitter seemed to harden, and the window suddenly became a significant barrier between them. She also noticed his strong hands clutching at the windowsill so tightly the knuckles were almost white. She let his words sink into her mind. She realized after all they were full of tension.

Thoughtfully, with all the well-modulated tones of a record, she said, "I wonder whether things just became like this or whether there was something else behind it. I mean, people do drift apart, of course, stop seeing each other, and the years go by and nothing happens, but something might have started it. You may never even know what. But there is still a reason."

She looked down and asked simply, "Do you think there's a reason?"

"No," Martin answered curtly and irritably. He stood still for a few seconds, frowning heavily and still grasping the sill, then he let go and straightened up, trying to look untroubled again.

"You'd better pack and start thinking about getting ready. You look terrible in those old overalls."

"So we're staying the night?"

"Christ, yes, we're staying the night. I have no intention of driving back tonight. But I'll phone the Werners and ask the boys to look after the stables until tomorrow."

He paused.

"Maybe I should give the horses maize, too—think they'd run better?"

He closed the window and vanished inside the room, and Ellen continued on her way to the kitchen door. Chatter, she thought. He's trying to chatter it away.

It worried her, but she did not know whether it had anything to do with Mauritz, or someone else, or the past, or something in the future. All she knew with any certainty was that Martin had something very unpleasant in his right inside pocket, an object that until this moment she had never guessed was in the house. A menacing little object. It was a pistol.

4

MELANDER

MELANDER, THE CHIEF OF POLICE, LIVED IN A HOUSE ON THE outskirts of Gislaved's white-collar district. Inspector Bertil Durell (senior salary scale) was standing in the middle of Melander's kitchen, his normally pink, fair-skinned face at the moment the scarlet of a ripe apple, contrasted by the startling ginger of his freckles and cropped hair. His suit was light blue with dark blue stripes, his shirt also blue, and across its faint pattern, a crazy tie of emerald green, orange, black, and pink swirled down between his lapels. The color scheme was rounded out by a pair of blunt-toed, shining ox-blood shoes.

". . . beautiful mooooorn . . . ing . . . ooh, what a beauti-fuuul day . . ."

He made a wide, sweeping gesture toward the open window, through which a flood of light shone onto the linoleum. Blinded by the glare and the generosity of the August sun, he closed his eyes and allowed his clear tenor voice to fill the whole room.

Melander listened appreciatively, cracking his breakfast egg and wondering what passersby might think of this morning serenade. Durell was staying with him for a few days while his loathsome—in Melander's opinion—aunt had her usual week's vacation with old friends in Halmstad. He liked Durell's singing and was sufficiently musical to realize that if this fat little man had not become a policeman, he would undoubtedly have had a career in opera. Not least impressive was Durell's repertoire. He had mastered most of the great parts in the major works, as well as innumerable dashing songs of profane as well as spiritual literature.

Melander filled his spoon with runny egg yolk and inserted it between his thin lips, wondering absentmindedly why a police car had stopped outside his back entrance. For a moment it crossed his mind that a neighbor might have reported the noise coming from the police chief's house, but he immediately abandoned the thought as too absurd. No one could object to someone celebrating such a lovely Sunday morning with such splendid singing, and there was certainly no call for police intervention. Yet he signaled Durell to stop.

The little inspector slowly closed his mouth and the last note died away in a surprised pianissimo.

"You didn't like it?" he asked.

"Yes, of course," Melander said apologetically. "But your breakfast—your egg's getting cold. Have a seat . . ."

He looked out the window again. The car door opened and slammed shut, and one of his deputies walked toward the house with a stranger beside him, a slight, vigorous, middle-aged man in a well-cut suit. Melander found himself trying to recall whether he had seen him before. Then there was a knock on the door and before he could swallow his egg, the door opened and both men came in, the deputy looking slightly embarrassed.

"This man has something to report," he said. "Something's happened out Våthult way—at old Miss Lethander's place."

"Oh. Yes?" said Melander, looking questioningly at the well-tailored man.

"My name's Corn," he said. "Mauritz Corn. I'm a relative

of Miss Lethander's and am here to celebrate her ninetieth birthday. It's today. We—well, the telephone's cut off, so I had to drive here to report—that is—I think the police had better look into this right away."

"This?"

"Yes. I drove straight to the police station, and they sent us here. We haven't been able to get hold of a doctor, either. I think you'd better arrange that, too."

He paused.

Melander got up from the table, rattling the china. "My dear man, just what the hell is all this about?"

The other man stiffened, clearly not used to being addressed that way, and not liking it.

"There are two dead people out there at the moment," he said. "And I can't say for sure but I think it's a question of murder and suicide. I'm not personally involved, but naturally it's always unpleasant when such things happen."

"When was this discovered?"

"Just before I got there. I drove down from Stockholm overnight. The situation was—how should I say—chaotic. Especially since the telephone was out of order and no one could sound the alarm. So I drove straight to the police . . ."

Melander frowned. "All right," he said. "We'll go there immediately. I just hope a whole lot of people haven't messed things up for us before we get there. Murder and suicide, eh?"

Mauritz Corn nodded. "Looks like it. But don't worry about things being disturbed. The bodies are in separate rooms, and the rooms are locked. No one could possibly forage around without first forcing the doors, and I've personally told them not to. Anyhow, the only person who might have done such a thing is lying just inside one of the doors. His name was Martin Bernheim, the owner of Björnholm Manor. Perhaps you know him?"

Melander nodded.

"Yes, I know Martin Bernheim."

But Durell was thinking about something else as he sat there looking at his uneaten soft-boiled egg. He was thinking about the way in which Mauritz Corn had expressed himself.

"His name was Martin Bernheim," he had said. "Was," not "is." Durell sighed. The man must have been dead as far as Mr. Corn was concerned for a very long time.

5

ULLA

To Ulla, everything seemed to be taking place in a fog. She could see and observe, but she couldn't really grasp anything. The house was suddenly full of people—police, doctors, photographers—and the family, all of them. At first there had been only three policemen—the driver, then a small fat man in blue, and then Melander, the chief constable. She called him that, even though she knew the title was different nowadays. She remembered him well and thought he hadn't changed a bit. Tall and sinewy, and with such short jacket sleeves that half his lower arms protruded. But even though he was tall, he still had to climb onto a stool to look through the glass pane at the top of the door into Martin's room. He stood there looking for quite a while, then slowly shook his head and said something to the short man, who also got up on the stool, but still couldn't see, and had to ask someone to get a stepladder. Alma and Carl got it, and while they were putting it up, Melander moved the stool over to the other door, stood up on it, and stayed there for a long time. The small fat man made a corresponding inspection from the stepladder, first of Martin's room, then of Victor's. When they had finished, they conferred together. Ulla overheard the words "shot" and "carbon monoxide."

Suddenly Alma's voice cut through the fog with crystal

43

clarity. "Yes, I lit a fire for Mr. Martin while the young people were dancing downstairs."

As she stood there Ulla heard the church bells again. Just like the day before, but now they were ringing for morning service. Yesterday they had been ringing in the Sabbath . . .

"Can you hear the bells ringing in the Sabbath?" Ulla asked.

She went over to the window, opened it, and let the sound of bells from Våthult's twelfth-century church float into the room. She couldn't make out the church, but she remembered how it looked over there on the other side of the lake, and she knew it was white and ancient and that some of her ancestors were buried beneath old iron crosses in its churchyard.

Large blue-black clouds were piling up on the horizon, like immobile giants illuminated by the sun, and she thought vaguely that thunderclouds always looked blacker when the sun was shining on them. The sight of the dead, calm mirror of the lake, the unmoving branches of the birches below, the close, warm air that fanned her face as she opened the window, and the tolling sound of the bells all oppressed her, and for the third time that day painfully brought back her headache—even though she had taken two powerful pills after lunch. She heard Fredrik coming up behind her, standing just far enough away so as not to touch her but just close enough so she could smell liquor on his breath.

"Shut the window," he said. "I detest that bell ringing."

She did as he had asked.

"I think there's going to be a thunderstorm," she said. "That dreadful headache's creeping up on me again. I'll have to take another pill."

"You should stop taking them," he said. "Hell, you gobble a bottle a day, and you took one less than an hour ago." He sounded decisive. "You took one when the old bitch came back from her walk. Right, Carl?"

He turned to Carl, who was lying on the sofa reading. Carl didn't even look up.

"That was when you went down to the pantry for the second time," Carl said. "I guess it's time for another trip, huh? I can tell from your tone of voice." He gave a nasty little laugh. "Mother has her pills and you have yours. Here, I'll get them for you . . ."

He closed the book, raised himself awkwardly off the sofa, and walked over to Ulla's handbag, which was on the bureau. He extracted a bottle of pills, which he held up to the light, inspecting it with interest.

"Oho, strong stuff."

Then he unscrewed the lid and peered into the bottle with one eye closed.

"Nothing, nothing there."

He shook the bottle in the air and dropped it in the handbag, the white plastic lid after it, then spread out his hands in a gesture of apology.

"All gone," he said. *"Alles weg. Finis."*

Fredrik let out a bellow of laughter and turned to stare at Ulla, his feet apart and his hands on his hips.

"Was that the bottle I bought for you the other day? On that old prescription you said would last you at least two years?"

Ulla was terribly confused.

"That's impossible," she said. "They can't be all gone."

She sank into the chair that was conveniently just behind her, knowing that Fredrik had probably emptied the bottle because he didn't like her taking them. But she did not dare to ask. He might be furious, because when he'd had a few drinks, it was awfully easy to upset him. As she sat there in confusion and doubt, Fredrik walked over to the mirror. He buttoned his shirt up to the neck, but did not bother to put on the tie hanging on the back of the chair beside him. He stretched, then looked at himself carefully to make sure everything was in order—or at least that he looked as if everything were.

"I'm going to see her now," he said. "She can't still be napping."

Ulla thought he was simply trying to avoid questions about the bottle of pills. That was why he had chosen this particular moment for his mission, and it worried her because the timing was so inappropriate.

"You shouldn't go alone," she said. "I'll come with you. She's always listened to me, and she's always been slightly suspicious of you. And I know if she won't listen to you or if she simply says no, you'll only be angry—especially now . . ."

"What d'you mean, especially now?"

He swung around and glared at her.

"Now that you've been drinking."

"That's ridiculous. I'm going. Alone. You've got a headache, right? I'm not going to ask her for any favors, so why should she refuse? It's a question of being treated fairly like the rest of the family. And let me tell you, if she puts up a fuss, she'll have me to reckon with."

"That's what I'm afraid of, Fredrik dear," said Ulla faintly.

But when he went out, she made no effort to follow him, for she knew it was pointless to argue.

Carl picked up his book and headed for the door.

"Don't worry, he won't go," he said, shrugging his shoulders. "He just wanted an excuse to slink down to the pantry for another whiskey. You never seem to learn."

He went out of the room and Ulla was left alone with her headache.

She crossed the room and sat down on the sofa, her whole body tingling with anxiety. Carl was probably right—Fredrik had gone off for another quick one. On the other hand, it was not out of the question that he had gotten up the courage to see Aunt Charlotte. He had certainly talked about it for long enough, he had to have the money, and Ulla had in fact encouraged him, although deep down she was very uneasy. But if he went to see her now, she was sure the old lady would smell the liquor and be offended, or at least unwilling to discuss anything at that moment, though perhaps she would on another occasion when Ulla was there. Ninety today. Supposing the subject had been brought up far too late? In that case it was probably mostly her fault, because she lacked the courage. Fredrik had nagged her more than ever about it recently. Basically, that was what had made him decide to come down. As he always said, although they were in no actual need, it was wretched to be dependent on other people and on the state of the market, which made it impossible, so to speak, to shape one's own destiny. He was not too old to start his own business, as long as he could get some financial backing, and as far as he could see, there might be a possibility of a loan.

Ulla stayed where she was, her thoughts swirling around in her head. She sat there for a minute, then two, then five . . . Her anxiety grew steadily worse, but to her surprise and relief, her headache receded. Finally she could no longer bear doing nothing. She picked up her handbag and opened it, automatically taking out the bottle of pills and throwing it into the wastepaper basket. Then she left the room. She noticed to her shame that she was almost slinking along the corridor to the hall and past Martin's room. The door into the dining room beyond was closed, but she nevertheless imagined the long stretch through the dining room and then the long corridor on the other side leading to Aunt Charlotte's private apartment. The very thought of the long way she had to go, and her resolve to help Fredrik with the old lady, made her feel weak at the knees.

She stopped suddenly. She could hear voices coming from Martin's room, though she knew Martin wasn't back yet from the manor. She recognized the voices. The loudest and most blustering voice was Fredrik's, and the teasingly calm and controlled one was Victor's.

"We'll put a stop to that," said Victor. "Martin and I'll take care of that. You can bet on it."

"You'll put a stop to it!" Fredrik's voice was boiling with

anger. "You won't stop anything. I'm going to crush both you and your father, in my own time and in my own way."

The next moment, the door opened and Fredrik came out flushed and seething with rage, his arms swinging. In his blind fury he never even saw Ulla, but strode across to the great staircase and disappeared between the heavy oak banisters.

She had stood there breathlessly, on the same spot where she was now standing watching one of the policemen fiddling with the lock of the door, until he gave up on it and said, "There's nothing we can do except unscrew the hinges and lift the door off."

While they were doing it Ulla returned to her musing. She thought about the unfortunate blunder Fredrik had made last night during the party, when he had squabbled with Aunt Lethander, and about the spat in the kitchen between the young people, and how Charles had come rushing out with a swollen lip. And then, of course, about what Charlotte had said about the shot that morning, how she had heard a shot last night, though at the time she hadn't realized it *was* a shot. Heavens—who would have expected that? Even the police had to see that.

6

DURELL

DURELL WAS STANDING IN THE MIDDLE OF THE ROOM BY THE open fireplace, looking thoughtfully up at the ceiling where the cone-shaped flue vanished into the plaster. Then he bent down under the cone, trying to extract a hidden secret from the dark, circular hole, but all he saw was a sharply defined circle enigmatically and dismally staring back at him with its sooty black eye.

He straightened up and drew a line with red chalk on the white cone to mark the position of the damper.

Over by the broad bed, the police doctor had just cut the clothes from around Martin Bernheim's powerful body, which was lying, relaxed and peaceful, on top of the bedspread. Durell walked over to the group of police officials working there. The photographer—snapping photographs of the body; the objects around it; the windowsill, on which the pistol still lay; the dressing gown over the back of the chair, in the pocket of which Melander had found the key that fit the door to the other room. Melander—industriously jotting down notes on a pad, examining the window, running his eyes over walls and ceiling, bending down to look at the remains of the fire that had burned in the fireplace and sealed Martin Bernheim's fate. The doctor—dictating his observations quietly into a pocket tape recorder: "high-grade rigor

49

mortis—as expected from carbon-monoxide poisoning—
bright pink to almost red complexion—body apparently
undisturbed since death—no sign of external violence—position of body indicates . . ."

The monotonous voice faded beyond Durell's thoughts. As
always when confronted by sudden death, he was filled with
wonder and melancholy, but at the same time he also felt
some of the excitement of the hound's eagerness to track
things down, seek out the truth, analyze the indefinite scent
from the drama, and elucidate the whole situation in an un-
assailable report. He listened to Melander's voice with professional approval as Melander told two younger policemen
they should never take anything for granted, they should
make sure they missed nothing, that details were important,
and even if it was clear this was suicide, they were not to forget that what had taken place in the next room was murder.

Yes, what had taken place in the next room had been
murder. Victor Bernheim was lying on his back with his eyes
open and lines of surprise around his mouth. The bullet had
gone straight into his heart, through the top pocket of his
light jacket, through the top pocket of his bright red shirt,
where it had simultaneously passed through a piece of paper
folded in four. The paper was slightly bloodstained around
the bullet hole, but was otherwise perfectly legible. From the
typewritten information the paper contained, it appeared
that Victor was expected to pay a gambling debt of fifteen
thousand kronor within a week of the date on the letter—
which gave him three days to go—and if this were not done,
he could expect to be ruined. The signature was hardly legible, but Durell concluded that young Mr. Bernheim almost
certainly knew who the sender was and to whom the money
was to be paid.

He had evidently been sitting in one of the small armchairs by the center table when the murderer had pressed the
trigger. Certain signs indicated that he had gotten halfway to
his feet the moment before the shot went off, then had fallen

back again, knocking over the chair he had been sitting in. A little blood had trickled onto the pink carpet, which also showed that when he died, he had fallen into the position in which he now lay. There was nothing in the room to indicate trouble or a fight before the murder. There was a camera on the table that, upon examination, turned out to have no film in it. But an exposed roll of film was found in the briefcase by the bed, along with another roll of unexposed film. The briefcase appeared to be untouched, as was the still-packed suitcase containing various clothes and articles one would expect to find in a suitcase whose owner had planned to be away for a few days. One detail might possibly have been worth noting, and that was a pair of slightly muddy footprints just inside the door. The pattern, faint though it was, indicated that they came from a pair of running shoes, but identification would be difficult. What they nevertheless could be certain of was that the footprints had not come from the shoes found on Martin Bernheim's body. The footprints had probably appeared on that sensitive carpet sometime before the murder and were almost certainly of no importance to the case.

The course of events appeared to be quite clear. In his mind Durell pictured the older man coming into the room with the pistol in his pocket. The younger man suspected nothing and had calmly remained seated. But at that stage the decision must have already been made, for otherwise why would the murderer have a weapon with him? Naturally his intention might have been simply to threaten his son with it, but Durell did not believe that. When two people so closely related meet with a weapon involved, it is bound to be deadly serious. Father and son. The son killed. Usually it is the other way around. Well, maybe there was an argument before the shot was fired, but hardly heated enough to worry the younger man or even make him suspicious. No, the other man seemed to have been well prepared for what had surprised the son. From long experience, Durell knew people seldom remained seated at a table when confronted with an unexpected and threatening situation. Faced with the unexpected, people lose their confidence. Remaining calmly seated showed confidence. Was that what the younger man wanted to show his father? Confidence? Perhaps the lack of confidence had been in the father. In that case the question was why? Perhaps there was an answer to that question.

After he fired the shot, what had the murderer done? Everything was crystal clear, Durell thought. The murderer had finished a prearranged plan. He hadn't even tried to conceal the murder by arranging it to look like suicide. That could have been done. No, Martin Bernheim understood what he had done, what he had felt forced to do, and he was also going to take the consequences. He knew he couldn't go on living with this. He had taken the pistol with him, left the room, locked the door on the outside, taken the key with him, gone into his room, and locked that door, too—on the inside, of course. Then he had closed the damper on the fire burning in the open fireplace, put the pistol on the windowsill, and sat down on the bed and waited. Carbon monoxide— it usually did not take very long, a few minutes, perhaps, at the most a quarter of an hour. The inspector's pale blue eyes went blank, but inside his head a large question mark kept appearing after almost every link in his chain of thought.

He sighed and spoke to Melander, who had just started examining the heap of ashes in the fireplace. "You've already noticed, right?" he asked quietly.

Melander looked up. "Noticed?"

"That the damper's open."

"No, I haven't got that far yet. But that was obvious the moment we came into the room."

"Carbon monoxide. How could he have killed himself if the damper wasn't closed?"

Melander smiled. "Maybe he changed his mind and managed to open the damper again before he became so groggy he had to go and lie down? The dose he'd already had would've been enough."

"What does the doc say?"

Durell closed his left eye as he looked at the police doctor.

"Well, it's possible," said the doctor. "But I doubt he'd have managed to close the damper if he was already feeling that bad. I suppose it takes quite a while before the room is aired, even if the damper is opened again. He could have been poisoned."

Durell nodded. "But *why* should he change his mind? His motive was obvious the moment he'd killed his son. He couldn't undo that. It was logical of him to complete it."

"I doubt people think logically in such situations."

"No, but if he changed his mind, why didn't he open the window before opening the damper? Or after opening the damper?"

"Don't ask me," said the police doctor, smiling wryly and throwing up his hands. "But I know you sometimes find people who suddenly realize they're being poisoned by carbon monoxide and have managed to get to the window, maybe to open it, but then they can't manage it. They simply don't think of breaking the glass. You know, people don't think very clearly in these situations."

"But in that case they've been surprised, haven't they? They suddenly discover something's wrong. But in this case he *knew* what it was all about."

Melander nodded, carefully brushing the remains of the ash into a plastic bag. "Maybe. Let's think about it, my friend. Let's think about it."

Durell smiled at his tone of voice, which reminded him of a sorely tried mother calming her impatient child.

"It could be a double murder," said Durell.

Melander turned around and looked at him in astonishment. "What makes you think that?"

"But perhaps it couldn't be, of course, since this door was locked from the inside."

"Exactly," said Melander. "And when you were in the other room a moment ago, we found the key to *that* door in the pocket of the dressing gown hanging over there."

He gestured toward the claret-colored velvet gown on the corner chair.

"Yes, I thought it'd be in here," said Durell thoughtfully. "Couldn't the key have been turned from the outside? With a small pair of pincers, for instance?"

He went across to the door and examined the key closely, without touching it.

"Are there any traces on this key?"

His pale blue eyes were directed at the young technician who had just come in from Victor's room, where he had been looking for fingerprints and fixing them.

"Nothing special on the key. Should we take it with us?"

"Yes, take it," said Durell. "But what do you think? Could it have been turned from the outside with some clever instrument?"

The technician shook his head. "Doubt it. Anyhow, the hasp was on, too."

Durell was taken aback. Only now did he notice that there was a staple on the door down by the floor and a corresponding hasp on the doorpost.

"Are you sure the hasp was on?"

The technician nodded slightly disparagingly. "It was on."

"Well, that's that," said Durell, hesitating for a few seconds, but then he couldn't resist adding, "And do you think it would be possible to put the hasp on from the outside —with a thread or something? Through the keyhole, for instance?"

The other man's smile was now openly contemptuous. "No. There's a key in the keyhole, and it's on the inside and fills the keyhole so well there's no room for any kind of manipulation."

Durell nodded. "Then that means it'd be impossible to manipulate the *damper* from the outside in any way—for instance, closing it or opening it again?"

He got a shrug in reply from the young technician, and he also noticed that, over by the fireplace, Melander appeared slightly irritated by his obstinacy. But he refused to allow himself to be put off. Inside his head was a vague unsubstantiated and yet annoying sense that the course of events he had imagined, and which the others accepted, did not quite add up. He had had that feeling before, usually originating from some detail he had unconsciously noted and of whose full importance he had only later become aware. Or from a careless word, or a passing remark that at a later stage turned out to be of enormous significance. Or a circumstance that appeared quite innocent and therefore was neglected, but which from another angle became evidence of great importance. He made an effort to track down what it was that was wrong in this scenario. Everything was so perfect—apart from the damper being open. Everything tallied so well with the verdicts of murder and suicide. This was exactly how it should be for the report, with photographs and doctor's certificate, true deduction bordering on certainty concerning the course of events, the case written off and filed away. Yes, it was probably perfect. Durell chewed on the thought and suddenly realized what it was that did not add up. It was *too* perfect. Apart from the damper. Why was the damper open?

He turned to Melander.

"I may be wrong," he said. "But I'd still like to tackle this from a fresh angle."

The other man looked at him in bewilderment.

"I mean murder. Double murder. By a cunning murderer."

7

VERONICA

IN A FRIENDLY BUT DETERMINED WAY, THE POLICE REQUESTED that we go downstairs. Their request was necessary because the horrible discovery had given us a shock that was paralyzing. When the first door was taken off—the door into Martin's room—and we could see him in there on the bed, big and strong and not moving, I could hardly stand it any longer. I turned my eyes away and noticed Ellen. She was strangely composed as she stood there by the stairs with Vera beside her. Vera had her arm around Ellen's shoulders, as if to console her, but in fact Vera seemed to need support more than Ellen. It struck me as strange that Vera was crying, in a choked, stifled way, her arm around Ellen's shoulder jerking uncontrollably now and then. Vera had detested our father, hadn't she? And more than anything she had felt contempt for Victor. Why was she crying? In the frozen state I was in myself, that illogical question was the only one that occurred to me.

Ulla, Fredrik, John, and Charlotte were sitting in a small group around the old copper table by the door that led to the dining room. Fredrik kept whispering something to Ulla, looking as if he were about to get up and do something, but she stopped him each time. Beside them sat Mauritz and

Malin. He appeared fairly unmoved, and so did she, but what was actually going on inside her was hard to say. Malin seldom revealed her emotions. Her husband, the Yugoslav, had not appeared at all.

Charles, Gittan, and Carl were chatting over by the windows. It made me feel ill to hear one of them laugh. It sounded like Carl to me—a short, nasty little laugh that stung like a nettle—and then there was a giggle from Gittan. I turned around and looked at them. Gittan was on the verge of hysteria and Charles was squeezing her arm to shut her up.

I could barely see Aunt Lethander when I looked down the corridor, into the far end of her room. She was sitting there, far away, facing us, dressed in blue, in a blue chair with blue shadows all around her.

One of the policemen asked us to go downstairs and wait there. We obeyed in silence. Actually, it was not a question of obeying, only of fulfilling a wish we had felt all the time but that needed this impulse to become reality. Just as we were starting down the stairs the small fat policeman with ginger hair came over to us.

"We'd be grateful if you would stay downstairs," he said with a friendly smile. "To be at our disposal, as we usually say. Naturally we'll be grateful for anything you can do to help us shed some light on this matter."

We didn't stay downstairs. Ellen didn't want to. She asked us to go with her over to her wing, because she couldn't bear to be with the others in the house. When we came out onto the steps outside, the sunlight hit us like a warm curtain, but the heat scarcely penetrated my skin, I was so cold and frozen. The Yugoslav was sunning himself in the yard outside the other wing, his dark body glistening with sweat, his muscles like an anatomical chart. I thought he looked like a powerful, supple animal, an impression reinforced by the way he bounced out of the deck chair and bowed to us with a smile, just as he had done the day before when Aunt Lethander and Alma had gone out for their walk. As we were going indoors

Malin came down the front steps, almost dancing down them, and over to her husband, and when she reached him, she bent down and kissed him.

We had been indoors for almost three hours. Alma brought us a lunch tray, but we could only poke at the food and finally Vera put the tray out in the kitchen so we wouldn't have to look at it. Although we were isolated, we could sense the activity in the house. Another vehicle drove up to the front of the house. It was a ladder truck. It parked by the wall of the house. Not counting the ladder truck, there were now at least ten vehicles parked in front of the house and beyond the gateposts, two with the magical word POLICE on their sides. That word had always given me a sense of security when I had seen it before, meaning I wouldn't be molested walking home through Humlegård Park, or peace and quiet in the subway station. But now it was menacing. Now it confirmed that this whole horrible business was reality. Then there was an ambulance, a doctor's car, and a bus like one of those mobile recording studios the radio engineers use. That also belonged to the police. With all the other cars there, Victor's red sports car, Martin's Mercedes station wagon, Aunt Lethander's ancient Volvo, Mauritz's 244 model of the same make, and Malin's Saab, it was like looking at a public parking lot.

Three hours later, two policemen came out carrying a covered stretcher, which they brought over to the ambulance. I shuddered and wondered which one of them it was, and Vera turned away from the window. Ellen did not see it, since she was sitting far inside the room. They went back into the house but came out again five minutes later with the other stretcher. Strangely enough, I didn't think that one was Martin, but I was almost sure the first one had been Victor. The ambulance driver closed the back doors and jumped into the driver's seat. One of the policemen got in, too, and the ambulance started off down the narrow gravel road. A few moments later, the chief of police, Melander, came out with that ginger-haired freckled man with the hideous tie. They stood staring up at the façade of the house, which was covered with creepers. The short man was gesticulating, pointing up toward the roof, first to the left and then to the right. Then they disappeared around the corner of the house and reappeared a few minutes later on the other side. Melander went into the house again and came back with the ladder-truck driver, who jumped in and made the ladder rise up toward the chimney. Then another policeman came out. He had a bag in his hand but, despite it, climbed nimbly and lightly up to the roof, set his bag on a ledge above the window, and started some kind of inspection, the purpose of which I didn't know. He examined the roof around the base of the chimney, then got cautiously up on the tiles and painstakingly examined the upper part of the chimney. Meanwhile, the others stood down below watching his activities with interest. He did not come down for at least a quarter of an hour. The other men started bombarding him with questions and the short fat man took out a notebook and made one or two notes. Finally the short man threw up his hands, almost apologetically, put his notebook back in his inside pocket, and exchanged a few words with Melander. Then he spun around and headed straight toward us. I left the window, but as I turned I noticed Malin and the Yugoslav had disappeared, leaving the deck chair behind outside their wing.

Ellen opened the door and the small policeman stepped in, bowing slightly as his eyes surveyed the interior as if he were more interested in that than in us. Then he said quietly, but in a voice that was clear, "I'm an inspector in the Criminal Police and my name is Bertil Durell. Would you mind if I asked you some questions?"

Ellen nodded. She was still standing in the middle of the floor, next to him.

"It was your husband," he said. "And your son."

They were not questions, only statements.

She nodded again and started to speak. "It's . . ." Her voice broke, so she had to start again. "It's all so unreal."

"Yes," he said gently. "It's a horrible story. They're always horrible stories, these things."

"So you think Martin shot Victor, then took his own life?" she asked.

"Maybe—yes. Much points to that."

"It couldn't be so."

Ellen's voice was suddenly harsh in a way I'd never heard before. She went on without allowing time for the question I instinctively thought he was going to ask.

"Martin would never commit suicide."

"We know so little about each other. You don't believe he would be capable of killing his own son, either?"

"Yes. But not himself. He was not the kind of person to take his own life. He was much too positive—toward everything. And he thought far too much of himself to have done such a thing. Perhaps someone else, but not himself. And Victor—I hadn't expected it to be Victor at all."

Durell's eyebrows shot up and he looked astounded. "Expected?"

"Yes."

Ellen looked around uneasily, almost in confusion, I thought, avoiding the policeman's eyes.

"I thought something might happen—something unpleasant. But not Victor, and not anything like this—nothing so terrible."

"What did you think might happen—and to whom?"

She swallowed. "Mauritz. My nephew. The man who brought you here."

"Oh, yes. But why did you expect something to happen to him?"

"I don't know. Before we drove here yesterday, late in the afternoon, I found out my husband was preparing for this, preparing to meet Mauritz again. They hadn't met for many years. Martin had avoided—had always avoided talking about Mauritz. He hasn't mentioned—he never mentioned his name. But yesterday he prepared himself for the meeting."

"What do you mean, Mrs. Bernheim?"

Ellen's face was a grayish hue. She seemed to be struggling with an acute inner pain, and yet her words were controlled and her eyes almost coldly calm. The fact that she kept stopping, or hesitating, exchanging words, clarifying things, largely seemed to be so she could give herself time to think. So it was almost a shock to me when she replied calmly to Durell's question.

"He took a pistol with him. I presume that was what he shot Victor with?"

Durell nodded. "The pistol, yes. So he took that with him because he was going to meet Mauritz, you say. But he used it on his son."

"It seems so."

"Was their relationship that bad?"

"Not really. But something might have happened. Martin is very hot-tempered—he is—was—very impetuous."

"And yet," said Durell, as if to himself, "and yet this all seems so premeditated. Not passion—not manslaughter."

All these questions and answers built up more and more heavily inside me, and I felt I would break down if I wasn't allowed to say what I knew. It had been oppressing me all day. I'd wanted to tell Vera and Ellen but hadn't been able to. I knew what lay behind it all. Now the words came pouring out of me in a great flood that had been dammed up by my discovery that morning, dammed up by shock and my inability to speak without accusing, and by consideration and fear of the inevitable consequences of relating what I had witnessed the day before, when Victor had gone up to Martin and almost forced me to go with him. Now I poured it all out, that Victor had tried to extort money out of Martin, that he had incurred a gambling debt, that he had shown Martin that paper and threatened him with some letter that Martin had immediately known about, that he wanted fifteen thousand, that Martin was going to tell him what he was going to do about it today, and about Victor's mocking "Stella, Stella, Stella . . ."

When I had finished, I sank back into the chair by the window feeling incredibly relieved, as if I had been allowed to hand over the responsibility to someone else and was now free.

The little policeman stared inscrutably at me for a long time, his fingers holding a cheap ball point upside down and drumming it lightly on the black notebook.

"Victor had a piece of paper in his top pocket," he said finally. "It was a threatening letter from someone we'll try to get hold of, and it was about a debt of fifteen thousand kronor that was to be paid within three days from now, or else . . ." He let the sentence fade away into an unpleasant thought. Then he went on.

"What kind of letter was he talking about?" he said. "And what does it mean, this Stella business?"

I swallowed before answering.

"It was a letter that must have come from Stella, and Martin was frightened other people might find out about it. It was obvious that Victor knew Martin would let himself be blackmailed . . . he'd stolen the letter from Martin's desk drawer—at least, that's the impression I got . . ."

"Where did he have the letter?"

"I don't know. He said he could get hold of it very quickly."

"How quickly?"

"Very quickly. I don't remember very well."

"I see. Who is Stella?"

"Stella was—" I got no further because Ellen interrupted me.

"Stella was Mauritz's wife," she said. "She's been dead for many years. I've suspected for years that there was something between my husband and Stella. We used to see a lot of each other in the old days. Mauritz and Stella used to stay with us over vacations. Until Stella died."

Durell listened thoughtfully, pursing his lips. "So that's why you thought the meeting between your husband and Mauritz—that's why he was prepared?"

"Yes."

"You thought he was going to kill Mauritz?"

"No, not like that. I thought he was frightened of the meeting and didn't know what might happen, so he wanted to be prepared for all eventualities."

"But a pistol . . ." Durell frowned. "Did you think he felt so threatened he might have to defend his life?"

"I don't know." Ellen sank back again. "I may be wrong. I may have imagined it all. Naturally it's possible he took the pistol with him because he was being blackmailed by Victor."

"That he might be going to kill Victor?" said Durell.

"Yes. No. I don't know."

Ellen suddenly covered her face with her hands and silently and shakily started crying. Durell waited, looking at her with compassion, then nodded to me, and I intuitively understood. I got up and went over to Ellen and started stroking her head to calm her. All this time Vera had been standing silently over by the window. Now she suddenly spoke.

"I knew Martin had had an affair with Stella," she said. "I saw them once. It was disgusting. I was coming out of the stable and heard them laughing in an empty stall. It was in the middle of the day, so I didn't think I would be barging in on anything. I was fifteen or sixteen. They didn't see me, but I saw them—saw them there in the straw, entwined and panting. Martin was talking all the time—a meaningless prattle of vulgar words pouring out of him—and then her sexy laugh that simply paralyzed me with disgust and fear and hatred. Then I crept out. I couldn't face going back to the house to Ellen. I remember she was fixing lunch. So I went out into the forest and walked and walked for hours, walking and running and resting, not getting back until late in the evening, and I remember crying that night until my heart seemed to break. From that day on I dreamed all the time about getting away from home . . . and from that day on I've hated Martin."

Vera fell silent as abruptly as she had begun. Then she laughed slightly apologetically and went on.

"I no longer think the affair so extraordinary. But it's strange to discover that whatever your moral values later in life, however free you may feel of irrelevant emotions or whatever, you still can't live with the kind of trauma an experience like that gives you without keeping within you a lot of the hatred and contempt you once felt. And it wasn't just the sex. It was because it was Martin. And it was straw and obscene words and obscene laughter . . . it was all so sordid."

When she had stopped talking, the silence was naked and horrible. Vera had spoken of something she should have kept quiet about. She had pilloried not only Martin but also Ellen. At least, that was what I felt. Ellen had stopped crying, and was now quiet and rigid beneath my arm.

The inspector had stopped drumming with his pen. He had listened with attention and perhaps some surprise to Vera's candid story, and now seemed to find it difficult to go on. But he didn't have to. Vera started walking back and forth across the room, her large glasses and cropped hair making her look like a lecturer searching for a good introduction to her next discourse. When she started again, she sounded as didactic as she herself always used to say she never wanted to be.

"This information about the pistol," she said. "It's interesting to analyze it, isn't it? First of all, it's possible Martin brought it with him to kill Mauritz, if he actually thought events might make that necessary. But it's also possible he was going to kill someone either in self-defense or on his own initiative. One has to ask oneself, Why did he think there was going to be a confrontation? Or why did he consider *at this moment* that he had any reason to kill Mauritz? Could Mauritz have been a threat to him in some way? I realize, Inspector, that you will have to devote some time and thought to that question. *If* the pistol was to be used against Mauritz at all. But now we know it wasn't used against him. It was used against Victor. So, second, we must ask whether he brought the pistol with him to kill Victor because of his attempt at blackmail—that fifteen thousand kronor, I mean. Or did he bring it because Victor had that letter from Stella and although he couldn't or wouldn't pay the fifteen thousand he simply had to have that letter back? But why did he have to have the letter back if he had been planning to commit suicide afterward? Wouldn't it have been just as well to commit suicide if he wanted to avoid the unpleasantness or threats the letter that Victor had entailed? Anyhow, it seems utterly preposterous that Martin should mind it all coming out—years afterward—that he had had an affair with Stella. It wouldn't be for our sake, anyhow, or for Ellen's. No, in that case the only thing I can think of is that it was for old Aunt Lethander's sake—*she* might have considered cutting someone out of her will for such a trifle. But that doesn't in any way explain why he should take his own life as well. Does it?"

Vera stopped and stood still in the middle of the room, looking at Durell.

"That's the way you police reason, isn't it?" she said.

Durell smiled slightly and, taking a deep breath, looked at her with approval. "Exactly. That's how we reason. I like your approach to the problem, Miss Bernheim. I am even slightly impressed. On the other hand, what you say is not entirely free of contradictions, nor is it exhaustive."

Vera shrugged. "I hadn't expected that. It's the principles I wish to get at, and since I've had slightly longer to think about it than you have, and since I actually know those involved better, I thought I ought to account for what conclusions I'd arrived at."

She stopped for a few seconds, then went on rather caustically. "Why isn't it exhaustive?"

"Because you accounted for two hypotheses but not the third. Perhaps Martin took the pistol with him to give it to Victor."

Vera looked at him for a long time.

"If Victor had received the threatening letter," he went on, "it isn't out of the question that his father would want to give him a weapon to defend himself with, even if it was used in another way. Is it?"

Vera looked gravely at him. "Maybe. But to return to the principle. All is not as it might seem. I'm beginning to see that you have come to the same conclusion I have."

Durell smiled. "You mean—that it wasn't suicide," he said. "That Victor was murdered and Martin was probably also murdered. That this is a question of a double murder . . ."

He paused, then added, "That was what you would have said, isn't it, Miss Bernheim?"

Vera nodded but did not reply. For a moment the inspector and Vera stood looking at each other in silence, it seemed to me almost as if with secret understanding. Then Durell swung around on his heel, put his notebook back in his pocket, and started to leave us. But after he had opened the door and was standing in the doorway with his hand on the handle, ready to close it behind him, he suddenly said to Ellen, "Just a couple more questions, Mrs. Bernheim. Didn't your husband have any keys of his own? Or do you keep them?"

Ellen looked at him in surprise.

"Of course he had his own keys."

"Where did he keep them?"

"On his key ring, of course. He always carried his key ring —in his pants pocket."

"I just wondered, because he had none on him when we found him. Then . . ." He hesitated and then asked another question, this time addressed to no one in particular. "This

Stella—Mauritz's wife. I understand she died a long time ago. How long ago was it?"

Ellen answered again. "She died six years ago. Almost exactly six years ago—in August."

"How did she die?"

"She died accidentally. I don't know the details. Ask Miss Lethander. I think she knows."

8

GITTAN

DURELL WAS SMILING WITH SATISFACTION AS HE LEFT THE WING building and the Bernheim ladies. He had certainly been given plenty to think about. Among other things, he had learned that Martin Bernheim had had at least *one* weighty reason for taking a pistol with him. He was being blackmailed, and by his own son. But there was more of interest: a dark passion in the past that might still be casting its shadow in the present; a key ring that should turn up in some unknown place; and last but not least, a certain young lady equipped with an attractive sharpness of mind.

He met Melander in the downstairs hall. The chief of police was also looking satisfied.

"There's nothing wrong with the telephone," he said.

"You mean he was lying?"

"No, no. Temporary breakdown. I telephoned the exchange to check. From nine o'clock last night until eleven today the line was dead after being struck by lightning a few miles away from here. There was a heavy thunderstorm last night."

"Over twelve hours—that's a long time."

Melander nodded. "I thought so, too, but they said it wasn't easy between Saturday and Sunday. The emergency service is not all it should be."

He put his hand into his jacket pocket and pulled out an envelope, which he handed to Durell. "Here are the photographs," he said. "One roll blank. This is the other. They're *very* interesting."

Durell opened the envelope, pulled out a number of color photographs, and slowly leafed through them, one by one. There were some of a racetrack, professionally taken and perfectly exposed, then some group photographs in which he recognized most of the people. The family members here now. He examined with special attention the tall, burly sunburned man with silver-gray hair. Martin. Although Durell's profession had made him rather thick-skinned, he felt melancholy as he looked through the photos. So this was yesterday, taken perhaps as a record for the family archives, as a souvenir of what was certainly a rare meeting. He went on to the next picture and looked for a moment with unconcealed astonishment, then whistled in a way that made Melander smile and nod in total agreement. Durell spent a long time on the photograph before moving on to the next one, only to find another like it, and then another, then another. As he went through the series, he said, "My god, it's that blond one, right?"

"Exactly. Those are posed photographs. She's stunning, the girl, isn't she?"

"Very well done," said Durell. "He was a skillful photographer. What's her name? I'm not sure I was ever told."

"Gittan Svensson. She's married to a sporty type—that blond guy she was with up there in the hall. Wonder if he knew about this."

Durell laughed. "You may well ask. I don't think he'd find it terribly amusing."

He stood there going through the photographs for a long time, then said decisively, "By all means let's attack this angle right away. It's got to lead somewhere. Let's go find the girl." He put the photographs back into the brown envelope, slipped it into his jacket pocket, then followed Melander, who was already heading for one of the rooms along the corridor. Melander had already learned his way around, knew exactly who was in the house, how they were related, and which rooms they inhabited, all of which had been registered clearly in his notes.

She opened the door so quickly at their knock that she might have been waiting just inside the door ready for them. But when she saw who they were, she stepped back, almost frightened.

"Oh, it's you . . . I thought it was Charles."

Melander nodded encouragingly. "Does he usually knock on your door?"

"No, how stupid of me. I wasn't thinking. He's gone out running, you see. He's always out running in the woods, or at all kinds of tracks and—he's a member of Fredrikshof Athletics Association."

Suddenly she looked frightened again. "Why do you want to see me? Well, come on in."

She backed into the room, lithely yet slightly listlessly. Durell looked her over with considerable pleasure. She had changed into a thin, close-fitting blouse with, as far as he could see, nothing underneath, and which was anchored by a couple of narrow shoulder straps, making her long, slender arms look even slimmer. Her white jeans swooped down like shiny snakeskin over her hips and legs, accentuating every detail of her delectable figure. She sat down on one of the beds and ran her hand uneasily through her hair, which was newly washed and soft.

Before either of the policemen could think up a suitably calming introductory question, she suddenly said, "Everyone calls me Gittan, but my name's really Sigrid. I don't really understand how I got mixed up in all this. I haven't done anything the police should worry about."

"Please," said Durell. "No one thinks you've done anything. We just want to know a little about yesterday. There was a party here, wasn't there?"

She transferred her great blue-green gaze to Durell. "Yes. Is that what you want me to tell you about?"

"We have to start somewhere."

She looked slightly worried. "There's not much to tell. We had a whole lot of stuff out in the kitchen—lots of goodies, which I can't eat anyhow because I put on weight so easily. But the others ate, of course—they helped themselves out there and then we just sat around. Then they drank a lot, liquor and wine, and then the others went out into the hall, and upstairs, of course, and then we danced—not the old people, of course, but the rest of us—Victor and I and Charles and Malin and Veronica and Vera and—no, Vera didn't dance—and then Sergej. We used Carl's radio—it's awfully good. It was good music. And then we had great fun with the balloons. We had one of those balloon dances, you know. You tie the balloons to your leg and then you have to try to stamp on them to burst them, and the person who keeps their balloon the longest wins, you see."

Her sentences ran on without pause and with no change in intonation, and she kept her eyes constantly on Durell. Yet she was not speaking quickly. There was the same touch of listlessness in her voice and words as in her way of moving. But Durell had an idea it was conscious, a deliberate listlessness she had found an effective complement to the powers of attraction nature had endowed her with. Suddenly she laughed. "Charles was dreadfully annoyed with me once or twice. He thought I was flirting too much. But, god, just because you happen to be married, you don't have to turn off all the boys, do you, and anyhow we've only been married for six months. We met in Majorca and he sure never stopped eyeing the girls when we were going together down there." She stopped, then said quite seriously, "Don't you think I'm nice looking?"

Durell nodded encouragingly.

"Well, then." She slipped in a tittering laugh and went on. "Sergej tried to dance close to me and I let him, but Charles

saw, of course, and was dreadfully annoyed. I don't understand why he should be jealous about that, because he knows
that dark gigolo type doesn't turn me on at all. But he didn't
dare hit him. Sergej used to be a boxer, I think. Anyway,
Malin said he was as strong as a lion and Charles started to
object, though Sergej . . . though Sergej didn't understand a
word. Oh, my, it was fun for a while. But then that awful
thunder started. We turned out the lights and sat watching
the lightning—and, well, then Victor was suddenly standing
behind me and started hugging me and it was dark so I don't
think Charles saw anything. And then . . ."

She fell silent again, biting her lovely lower lip. Durell
thought he ought to help her out, and he pulled out the
envelope, took the photographs out, and handed them to her.

"And how did this come about?" he said exaggeratedly
lightly.

She stared at the photographs. "Have they been developed
already?"

She looked up at him with obvious astonishment. He
smiled and nodded. She looked down at the photographs
again, leafing through them, apparently delighted. "They
came out awfully well."

"Yes, awfully well. But when were they taken? Would you
mind telling us when they were taken?"

"Oh, dear. You see—Victor's taken photos of me before.
We met at his sister's, at Veronica's, a few months ago. She's
got a fabulously exciting little boutique and I happened to
be there when Victor went there and he took to me at once. I
could see that. Then he asked if he could take some pictures
of me because he wanted to sell some to some magazine or
other. I didn't want to at first. But then I realized that he was
good at photographing girls and all that—so I let him. And
now—well, last night, that is—he wanted to do it again. When
he was standing behind me, when we were watching the
lightning, he whispered to me that he'd loaded the camera if
I had no objection. At first I didn't dare, but then I noticed

that Charles had gone off somewhere. He wasn't there, I mean, and Victor was being so nice to me, so I went with him. But *how* can they have been developed so soon?"

"Express service," said Melander dryly. "The police can do things like that sometimes. Where did he take you?"

"Oh. Well, he took me up to the attic. There are some lovely, cozy little corner rooms up there with furniture and couches and things. And he—he took me there. It was really awful, with flashes inside the room and outside in the dark, and I was dreadfully nervous all the time that Charles would find us, because he was bound to have noticed that we weren't down there, of course."

"Why were you nervous—for your own sake or for Victor's?" said Durell, in an apparently untroubled voice.

"Victor's, of course." She turned her great eyes toward him again. "Charles never does anything to me. He's still much too in love with me for that. But then I don't think he'd dare tackle Victor again after that business in the kitchen—earlier, I mean."

"Pardon?" said Durell.

She laughed delightedly. "Well, Charles was slightly annoyed with him in the kitchen because he'd been—well, he'd been a bit forward with me, as Charles called it, now and then during the day. It really started when he kissed me at lunch, though that was really only a little fun, you know. But then when he tried to push Victor up against the wall, Victor hit him a little and said something about how Charles shouldn't make a fuss because he knew karate, he said. Victor, that is. Poor Charles. He cut his lip on his teeth, so he looks really dreadful right now. But that was earlier, you see, before we started dancing. And nothing showed on his lip then, but today it shows."

"Oh, yes. And when did this photographing up in the attic occur?"

She rubbed her forehead thoughtfully. "About eleven, I think. Or a little later. We were up there for about a half hour. By the time we came down the party was over. Nearly everyone was gone, and only John and Charlotte were left, sitting in the dark by the window watching the lightning. Then I went to my room. Here, that is."

"And Victor?"

"I suppose he went up to his room. No, I don't know, actually. I think he went out to the kitchen first because he said he needed a drink. All that sort of thing was out there, and we just helped ourselves to whatever we wanted."

"So you came here."

"Yes."

"And where was Charles?"

"Charles and Carl were sitting in here talking. They were waiting for me, they said. But then, when I got back, Carl left."

"And had Charles figured out where you'd been?"

She smiled, her lips parting sufficiently for the even white teeth to show. "He didn't say anything. Anyway, I don't think he'd think of those small rooms up in the attic. If he had, he'd have come up. Try to sneak up on us. Well, then— then he went out."

"Went out?" Durell raised his eyebrows in surprise and swiftly exchanged glances with Melander.

"Yes. I told you he was crazy about running and all that. I undressed and crawled into bed, and he undressed. But then he put on his jogging suit and said he had to go out and run off all the liquor he'd drunk."

"In the middle of the night? Even though there was a storm? And it was raining, too, wasn't it?"

"Oh, yes. It was pouring. But he doesn't mind that."

"When did he come back?"

She gave a soft, confused toss of her blond hair and smiled faintly, as if apologizing.

"I don't know. I fell asleep right away. But of course he was in bed this morning. We were waked up this morning, you see. This whole business. That awful thing had happened by then."

Durell nodded grimly. "And the jogging suit? He's wearing it now, I suppose."

"Oh, yes."

She got up from the bed and snaked over to the wardrobe, opened the door, and looked inside.

"He's wearing it now. He always does when he's out running. Jogging suit and running shoes. And then, when he comes back, it's always the same old thing. Shower and clothes in the dryer."

Then, unconsciously, and yet as a reply to an unasked question from Durell, she added, "They looked dreadful this morning, his shoes, wet and dirty. But it's awfully good, that business with newspaper. He puts newspaper inside them and they dry quicker."

Durell and Melander left her in front of the mirror, apparently pleased with herself. She had had something to tell and she had been allowed to play a part. All the anxiety and uncertainty she had shown at first had clearly been unfounded. As they shut the door behind them she ran her hands down her cheeks with narcissistic tenderness.

She's a very beautiful girl, thought Durell, but not particularly profound. Then, aloud, he said mostly to Melander but to some extent to himself, "You know, that photographing in the attic? Do you think only photographing went on?"

Melander smiled.

"Mmm, I thought of asking," he said. "But then it struck me that it didn't have much to do with the case. The only thing is, it's possible she was a little disappointed we *didn't* ask."

9

MISS LETHANDER

THEY WENT UP TO THE LANDING ON THE SECOND FLOOR. Melander retreated to the rooms where the police were still working, where both Bernheim senior and Bernheim junior had met their fates, the doors of which had now been replaced for sealing. Durell turned off through the dining room and walked down the long oak-paneled corridor leading to Miss Lethander's private suite of rooms. He knocked quietly and considerately, then put his ear to the door so as not to miss her reply.

She was standing by the window with her back to him. The atmosphere in the room was awe-inspiring, making him feel as if he were about to step into a glass store, and would have to move carefully so as not to break anything. He waited. Her thoughts were evidently far away, for the seconds tripped by undisturbed on their delicate feet under the glass dome of the old gilded wall clock behind the group of sofa and chairs; one minute passed, then two. He waited another minute and went in.

She was wearing a deep blue dress Durell found in very good taste. Her silvery-white hair floated above the neck of the dress like a summer cloud in a clear morning sky. She was very small and her skin was translucent. He realized that she seemed to be trying to compensate for her smallness by wearing the high-heeled shoes he caught a glimpse of, blue, too, under the dress, which went right down to within a few inches of the floor. Suddenly she broke the silence and without turning around said, "Would you be so kind, Inspector, as to close the door behind you. Then you may come and sit in the yellow armchair. You are welcome to smoke if you wish to, but please do not drop ash on the carpet."

Durell smiled. Her voice was brittle but distinct, her speech totally free of dialect. He closed the door, walked to the yellow armchair, and sat down.

"Thank you, Miss Lethander," he said. "I don't smoke. I like singing and one has to choose—either to sing or to smoke."

She left her place by the window and went over to the desk, where she carefully arranged some papers, putting one sheet of paper into a file, folding another and putting it into an envelope. Finally she put a blue pencil back in the pen tray.

"I always write with a pencil nowadays," she said. "It looks much better with ink, but then you can't make a copy, and I always like to keep a copy of everything I have written. And I've never liked ball-point pens."

She got up again and moved over to the armchair opposite him.

"So you don't smoke, Inspector. I like the smell of tobacco smoke. Cigars most of all. Do you know, Inspector, Malin smokes cigars, although she's a girl. Have you met Malin?"

"No," he said. "I've been very busy."

"I understand. She's my young great-niece, the third generation. I'm very attached to her, although I was *not* especially pleased when she married that foreigner. She could have had anyone she liked, and she chose someone like that. Do you know Ustasja, Inspector?"

"Yes, Miss Lethander."

"That's where he comes from, the Yugoslav. There are a great many people from Yugoslavia in this area. Two of them were involved in that murder. Of the ambassador. Did you read about the murder of the ambassador, Inspector? Of course, Lieutenant Rosceff isn't like that, but all the same, I find it difficult to reconcile myself to Balkans. We've had a great many foreign visitors here over the years—Germans, Frenchmen, Englishmen, and even Americans when I was a child. But never Bolsheviks like this. Not even Hungarians . . ." She stopped suddenly. "You see Malin's a *red*. It's an unfortunate trend today that so many young people are red. I suppose you think I'm very reactionary."

Durell nodded benignly. "A little, perhaps. Everything changes."

"Yes, everything changes. And yet there are things that are unchangeable." She sighed and sat in silence for a few seconds before going on in an uneasy voice. "I'm convinced that both Martin and Victor were murdered. It's nonsense to think that Martin could have taken his own life. And with carbon monoxide. But no doubt you've already come to that conclusion."

"I'm afraid we must assume that," said Durell gravely. "But that isn't the only question to which we have to find the answer. How did the murderer get in and how did he get out? The room was locked from the inside, you see."

"Find the murderer first, and you'll be given the answer afterward." The old lady's voice was as sharp as a knife edge.

"We've started," said Durell. "But, you see, a great deal has to be sorted out first. Most of our murderers come weeping to us and tell us voluntarily, but so far no one has come forward in this case. So we'll have to look for ourselves." He paused briefly. "Today is your ninetieth birthday?"

"Yes," she said, nodding and sighing. "Do you want me to tell you about my family," she went on slowly, "so that you become more acquainted with them all? I have to tell you that the family is very disparate, only alike in one particular aspect, and that is in their eagerness to inherit my money. I have no natural heirs—thank goodness, I must say, because it's better that people who wish one dead are not too close to one. My relatives are all on my brother's, Erik's, side. Are you interested in this, Inspector?"

He nodded encouragingly and she sank back into the armchair, which almost swallowed her up, she was so small and delicate. The arms of the chair were uncomfortably high and she did not use them, placing her hands in her lap instead and locking her fingers together. The blue dress, the armchair's yellow upholstery, the white hair, and the rosy transparency of her complexion made an elegant color scheme. She half closed her eyes and started talking, more or less to herself.

"My brother, Erik, had three children—Eva, Ulla, and Ellen. Eva was the oldest. She and her husband were killed in a road accident in Germany, poor things. Their son, Mauritz —Mr. Corn, who is a company director—has looked after my affairs for many years now. And Malin is his daughter. That's the senior branch, and I like them very much.

"Then there's the middle branch. Ulla married a factory manager in Stockholm when she was at home-economics college. *I've* always thought it a *mésalliance*, even if he does call himself an engineer. I do not like him, you see, Inspector. And he doesn't like me. But I'm attached to Ulla and the children, especially Charles. He sends me Christmas cards. I've been told that Carl is also *red*. But he's talented. He was confirmed here, and the minister once told me that he thought the boy ought to go into the church." She pursed her thin lips. "I'm glad he didn't.

"Then there are the Bernheims. Ellen, that is. She married Martin Bernheim, who inherited the manor from his father, who was a good friend of my brother's. That was how the young people met. I like the Bernheims. There's always been plenty of life in them. Victor with his cars and girls, for instance, and Veronica, who's so pretty, and Vera . . . though she . . . I simply don't understand her ideas."

She fell silent, apparently mentally reviewing the Bernheims and nodding, smiling, and clasping her hands. Then she suddenly straightened up and grasped Durell's hand. "One thing you must know, Inspector, and that is that these three branches of the family—they can't *stand* each other. That was mostly why"—she smiled to herself—"that was mostly why I got them all here for my ninetieth birthday. I thought that was an excellent reason and I had a definite aim in mind. When I asked them to come, they all came. All of them. Do you know why, Inspector? Well, when Charlotte Lethander has decided on something, then one obeys." She smiled with satisfaction.

"And do you know why one obeys? I'll tell you. The money. The inheritance. I have to tell you that expectations make for strong apron strings. When I snap my fingers, they come, even if they find the company unpleasant. Old Miss Lethander usually gets her way, and she also has quite a hold in places."

The smile remained there all the time, an indefinite curl of her lips, which Durell would not have called amused, as it might just as easily have been ironic or even inspired by malice.

She got up from the chair just as the clock struck four, and she paced the room in time with the striking. Durell looked around. This was her living room and study, where she presumably checked the bills every day, wrote her letters, did her embroidery, and read her novels. Time had stood still in this room, despite the pendulum. The carpets were yellow and gray and thick. Straight-legged nineteenth-century chairs with petit-point backs stood along the walls. There was a baroque table and an enormous cupboard stretching from floor to ceiling. The desk was mahogany with a letter rack and a double row of bookshelves. In the center was the group of chairs and the sofa with its row of embroidered cushions. An antique chandelier with innumerable yellowing prisms hung at either end of the room, and just beside the desk was a gray door of engraved mirrors. It was half open, and Durell caught a glimpse of airy curtains inside and the corner of a bed with white bedposts.

Miss Lethander paused by the window again, just as he had found her when he had come in. She said very gently, "Would you be so kind as to come over this way?"

Durell raised his eyebrows, but immediately got up and went over to her. He noticed that she scarcely came up to his shoulder, and yet he was not a big man.

"Look out there, Inspector," she said. "Isn't it beautiful? Unchanged."

He hardly needed to look because he already had some idea of how beautiful it was. Old Miss Lethander's room had a wide view across the valley, the lake beyond and then dark green rolling forest. On the way here he had seen the house from the road, from far away on the other side of the lake. The roof rose out of the edge of a steep perpendicular cliff. The building reminded him of a castle, its foundations of hewn stone, the brick walls behind thick creepers, the diamond-paned windows, steep tiled roof, and round towers at the corners. He thought she had used exactly the right word to describe both the view and the house itself— unchanged.

She seemed to guess his thoughts because she suddenly said, "My paternal grandfather built this house. I've lived here all my life. For ninety years, Inspector. But I used to travel a great deal in the old days, and I've always read the newspapers and kept up with what was happening, though rather from the sidelines these days. Some people are probably irritated by me sometimes. Because I obstinately stay on here in the house, I mean. There's a family mausoleum in the churchyard, after all." She sighed.

"I'm not thinking of moving anywhere else but there," she went on. "Whatever bright suggestions anyone cares to make. I've stood by this window for almost a century, watching the forest grow up and storms knock it down again, tree by tree. I've seen the shape of the lake change, the reeds spreading.

Unchanged, I said—well, as it's always been. A rhythm of its own, a life of its own, a struggle of its own. But that's only in this direction. It's like the past here. But otherwise around here there isn't a single spot that hasn't been affected. In the old days there were only farmers and smallholders here. Now there are manufacturers. Manufacturers of plastic rugs, manufacturers of brass buckles, manufacturers of sausage skins, and manufacturers of cigarette lighters for Volvo and Saab. Do you know what was here before the house was built, just where we're standing now, I mean? An ancestral precipice. It's been here since Viking days, though I don't suppose any Vikings lived here, you know, only cultivators. Nature is harsh. They fished, of course. The fishing has always been good in the lakes until the last few decades. There was salmon in the Nassa. And they hunted. I remember once . . ."

Her voice died away and she fell silent. He realized she was no longer talking to him but to herself, a monologue to the past. But when she had finished, she turned to him and said, "You know what an ancestral precipice is, Inspector?"

"Yes, Miss Lethander."

She smiled again, her face transparently thin-skinned, with its fine little wrinkles a tightly woven network that had caught up the brown spots of age. In the light from the window he noticed she had lightly etched the contours of her lips with lipstick. Her chin ran down into the taut skin of her neck, which was as wrinkled as her face. She had reached the stage of an eternal portrait and could hardly change anymore.

"Some of the old ones threw themselves down the precipice," she said. "Others were given help when they asked for it, and others were given help without asking for it. I wonder whether anyone would want to give me help without my asking for it."

He did not know what to say.

"I don't think—I mean, that would be rather drastic for our day, wouldn't it?" he said finally.

She laughed. "Why? For an ancient old hag it would be eminently suitable."

She grew serious again and went on. "Oh, yes, Inspector, there are probably those who would have no objection to giving me a helping hand."

For a while she again seemed to slip silently into herself.

"It takes courage to die," she said finally. "Perhaps that's why I've grown so old. Even if someone should wish to help me, perhaps that demands even more courage. We don't make use of ancestral precipices these days. The doctors are much more convenient, for instance, and it must be so unpleasant, of course, pushing old people over a precipice when the same thing can be done by being passive. By just waiting, I mean."

She put her hand on his arm. "Did you want something of me?"

Durell looked straight at her and asked the question undramatically: "How did Stella die?"

Miss Lethander did not reply at once. A faint shadow seemed to flit across her face and she turned her eyes away. Then, in a steady voice, she said, "Stella was staying with me in this house at the time. She had been here for almost a week. She had left Mauritz because something had come between them. Actually, I did not really like Stella very much. I was against the marriage from the start, since I thought she was far too loose-living and extravagant, so it didn't have so much to do with her being an actress, although many people thought that. Well, we got on better in time. And as I've always like Mauritz—Mr. Corn, that is—I gradually accepted it. But Mauritz was never happy with her. I always sensed that, although he never said anything.

"Well, she was staying with me that week in autumn, and Mauritz came down that Saturday, and then Martin suddenly showed up, too, unexpectedly. There were several heartrending scenes that Saturday, and Stella finally left the upstairs hall here and disappeared outside—at least we thought she had gone out. Gradually each of us went to our rooms. Mauritz was in the wing he's sleeping in now, and Martin was in his own room. But Stella didn't come back. We didn't find her until far into Sunday. And how long she'd been dead then, no one could say."

Durell looked at her questioningly. "Had she taken her own life?"

"We don't know. Perhaps it was an accident."

Miss Lethander gestured toward the window behind her.

"She was lying down there among the boulders. I remembered afterward that the window was unlatched and half open when I came into this room that evening. I closed it, of course, but I didn't realize. Stella fell down the ancestral precipice. It feels strange sometimes, having an ancestral precipice outside one's window. Do you understand that, Inspector?"

She walked over to the window again, and Durell sensed she wished to be alone. Before he closed the door, he saw her exactly as he had when he had come in, gazing out over the lake and the forest beyond, and the mountains beyond that; a blue-toned silhouette with silvery hair like a summer cloud, between dark green curtains.

10

ELLEN

Ellen tried telephoning the manor once or twice, in the hope that one of the Werner boys might be in the stable and would answer. One of Martin's practical extravagances had been to have an extension telephone out there. She was not certain what instructions Martin had left about the horses the day before, but according to their plans, they ought to have been back home several hours ago. She was also uneasy about the possibility of lightning having affected the hatchery. When she failed to get through on the phone, she decided to go check for herself. She asked Vera to drive.

"We'll go over and then come straight back again," she said. "I don't want to be alone over there—not as things are at the moment. I guess you and Veronica don't want to move there?"

Vera shook her head. "No, it'd be better if you stayed here. We've promised Aunt Lethander we'll stay until the end of the week. But I don't know now. Perhaps we'll leave earlier."

"All right, then. I'll have to ask the Werners to look after the horses until . . ." She stopped. "Well, until what? *I* can't look after them. I can't keep them. Are you ready?"

They went out to the large green station wagon, and Ellen got into the passenger seat while Vera hopped into the driver's seat. The key was already in the ignition. Ellen noticed, and was slightly surprised, because Martin was usually so careful about not leaving doors unlocked and always taking his keys with him. But what could happen to the car out here? Vera didn't notice, and she was usually quick to comment on anything concerning Martin.

They drove out onto the gravel road, swung off at the church, and came out onto the new wide concrete road that would take them to the manor in less than twenty minutes if Vera drove fast. She did.

Ellen leaned back. The dark pressure of what had happened and what was going to happen was constantly with her. The enforced company of relatives had been unpleasant, full of suspicion, envy, and antipathy. It had all started with the delicious buffet supper Alma had produced under Aunt Lethander's supervision. Ellen had been surprised when the old lady had been so generous with the liquor, almost as if making up for the moderation at lunchtime. Not content with that, she had even had a few drinks herself, at least a couple of shots and some red wine.

Both the upper and the ground-floor halls were decorated with balloons. On Aunt Lethander's instructions, Carl had found a whole box of decorations in the attic, which contributed somewhat to the gaiety of the atmosphere. At least with the young. They quickly cleared away rugs and started dancing, with the radio turned up far too high. The atmosphere brightened for the young but not for their elders, who sat around two tables in the downstairs hall. Fredrik Svensson immediately commandeered a comfortable armchair and placed beer, whiskey, and a heaping plate down in front of him on a small table he had clearly decided was to be for his own use. Every time he put down his glass Ellen noticed Ulla holding her breath; it was a beautiful little table with a polished top, and she was clearly interested in acquiring it in any future division of furniture. Martin and Ellen were sitting at the same table as Ulla, with John and Charlotte Bokström on the sofa next to them, and Aunt Lethander.

"Pity Mauritz isn't here. I'd have appreciated that," the old lady said suddenly.

Fredrik's face clouded over. He had hardly had time to drink more than one or at the most two whiskeys, but he was obviously drunk, so Ellen realized he had probably started drinking earlier in the day. Martin had evidently had the same thought, for he leaned over and whispered to Ellen, "Hope he makes a fool of himself."

His prayer was answered almost at once, for Fredrik said in a blurred voice, "You certainly have your favorites, Aunt Lethander. How many thousand has he acquired at our expense?"

"What do you mean, Fredrik?" asked Aunt Lethander.

The table fell deathly quiet; apparently not even the music was able to penetrate that barrier of silence. Ulla, gray-faced and rigid, sat with her mouth open. But Fredrik was not to be stopped. He straightened his large body and his hand fell so heavily on the delicate table that the glasses and plates jumped.

"I mean Mauritz has every opportunity of judging papers and that kind of thing, since he's in charge of your affairs. Bet you anything you don't look at those papers all that much yourself, trusting him as you do."

"What papers do you mean, Fredrik?"

"Well, you know, papers and things. Promissory notes and stock and mortgages and that sort of thing."

Ellen saw that Fredrik was on thin ice, but there was no stopping him. He drew another deep breath and out it came: "Not to mention your will. Where do you keep your will?"

"There's no need for you to worry about that, Fredrik," she said dryly. "It's in safekeeping. Since it's customary for the executor to take charge and ensure that the estate is divided properly, he'll have to wait awhile before going further into that problem."

"It'd be interesting to have some idea of the sum involved, anyhow," said Fredrik. "Wouldn't it?"

He looked around and Ellen looked around, but everyone was embarrassed except Martin, who looked amused.

Fredrik went on without waiting for a reply from Aunt Lethander. "I'm sure you've got quite a bit in the bank. Then there's this house. Do you have any mortgages on the house? Then there's quite a bit of land and forest and so on. But what about all the securities? How much is there in stock?"

Miss Lethander met his challenging look with an icy stare. "You must ask Mauritz, if it has anything to do with you, Fredrik."

But Fredrik was not to be put off. He took a gulp of the remains of his beer and growled ominously. "I and my family don't owe you a cent, Aunt Lethander. That's in writing—or, rather, there are no papers that say so. But what about Mauritz?"

He thrust his hand out vaguely in the direction of the dancers, who had clearly decided that the noisy monologue was disturbing them and were retreating toward the stairs up to the top hall, all except Malin, who was dancing with Victor but then freed herself from him and approached the older group.

Fredrik went on. "Mauritz's business—who loaned him the money for that? He didn't have any of his own to start with, did he? And what about you?" A large finger was suddenly pointed at Martin. "How much did you have to borrow to keep yourself afloat with all your horses and extravagances? And that boy of yours—what does he cost, may I ask? No, loans like that should be accounted for. That's only right, and everyone will be fairly and justly treated. We heard you say that at lunch. Tell us now—let's hear you call everyone to account."

Old Miss Lethander snorted irritably. "There are securities against what I have loaned to Mauritz."

"What kind of securities?"

"Stock."

"What kind of stock?"

"In his firm. It's a good firm."

Fredrik took in this information with staring eyes and half-open mouth, saliva collecting into two shiny lines in the corners of his mouth. For a moment he was quiet, as if he had not really grasped what had been said. Then he said craftily, "So we'll all be part owners of his firm, then? Do you know what it's worth?"

"You won't be part owners. They're preferred stock. The stockholders will be recompensed. Mauritz will redeem the stock."

"But for how much? And where's he going to get that money from?"

"That has nothing to do with me or you, Fredrik."

"Uh-huh."

Fredrik did not seem to have understood the reasoning, in fact felt he had been outmaneuvered and in some way made to look a fool. In revenge, he raised his voice and again turned to Martin. Ellen closed her eyes at the thought of Martin's possible reaction to such an attack.

"And what about you?" said Fredrik. "How much have you borrowed?"

"That's none of your business," snapped Martin.

"But you have borrowed some money?"

"Yes," said Aunt Lethander. "Martin has borrowed. Against securities, and there are mortgages on the forest. If he wants to redeem the mortgages or not, when they fall due, that's his business."

Fredrik was elated. He emptied his glass of beer and said firmly and heavily, to show he knew far more about all this, "If you don't redeem the mortgages, Martin, then we'll be owners of the forestland, too. But I'll demand that you redeem them, and then they'll have to be valued and auctioned if necessary—you never know, but in the end I might take my share of the forest. What do you think, Ulla?"

Ulla did not reply but wriggled uneasily without taking

her eyes off Aunt Lethander. Ellen realized how catastrophic this turn of events must seem to Ulla.

"Auctioned?" said Martin teasingly. "Do you think there'll be much left over if there is an auction, after all the claimants have taken their share? Take my house, and my horses, and Ellen's hen house, too, if you like, and every tree on my land. There wouldn't be much left for you, anyhow. The worst would be the other thing you would have taken."

"What other thing?" said Fredrik, looking bewildered.

"Honor—whatever that's worth. Yes, Fredrik. That's probably what Aunt Lethander meant at lunch today. Love, love, love . . ."

"Love, love, love—to hell with it," trumpeted Fredrik. "I need cash—it's *cash* I need, so I can start up on my own. If loans are being handed out willy-nilly, then, damn it, there must be something for me, too."

His hands fell to his sides, and, turning gloomily to Aunt Lethander, he said heavily, "Would you lend me twenty or thirty thousand? I want to start my own engineering firm, and I want to do it before I'm too old. If I wait too long, it'll never happen."

Aunt Lethander stared at him for a long while.

"No," she said finally. "You may not borrow any money from me, Fredrik. But if you like, you can go to the kitchen and fetch yourself another drink. And now this old bitch is off to bed. Good night."

She got up from the sofa and left them without another word. Fredrik stared after her in astonishment, saliva still glistening around his mouth, now matching a glistening in his eyes. He turned to Martin and hissed between his teeth, "That was your fault, you swine. You made me make a fool of myself. But I'll get back at you—you can be sure of that."

He disappeared somewhat unsteadily out into the corridor toward the kitchen.

Ellen saw the whole scene enacted before her eyes again. In retrospect, Fredrik's threat was clear. But Martin had not taken much notice then. He had let out a short laugh and got up and asked Malin, who had stayed at the table, to dance.

While they were dancing Ellen heard Martin say, "You've grown into a woman, Malin. Do you know you're devastatingly like your mother?"

Uneasily, Ellen watched them dance. She noticed Martin suddenly change tempo and dance at a slow pace to be able to hold her pressed close to him. Malin was almost as tall as Martin—when he pulled her to him, they were cheek to cheek. Ellen noticed something else, too. The Yugoslav. He was standing on the stairs glowering at his wife, but when he saw Ellen watching him, he started downstairs, crossed the hall, and disappeared out of the house.

"Diddled by one's own daddy, eh?"

Ellen started. Victor had come over to them and was smiling cynically as he sat down on the sofa in Aunt Lethander's place. Charlotte Bokström edged away slightly, as though the company were distasteful.

"You're not alone in that," Charlotte said. "He's going to diddle us, too."

Ellen felt a warm wave rise inside her. "What do you mean by that?"

"Well, out of our inheritance, I mean. Or some of the money. But we won't stand for that, will we, John?"

She nudged John in the side to get his support, or perhaps make him speak up. Ellen couldn't make out which. She thought the accusation was absurd.

"Why should he do that? And how would he be able to? Neither he nor anyone else can influence Aunt Lethander."

"Oh, yes, you know he can. You noticed how he got Aunt Lethander to leave. She doesn't even want to discuss it. We've talked about this, haven't we, John? You explain, John."

She nudged him again and John turned red.

"Well, it's like this. There wouldn't be much if that valuation came off and that kind of thing."

"That conclusion's probably correct," said Ellen briskly.

"But as inheritance and money on the whole do not play such an important part in the values of the Bernheims as they do to the Svenssons, I don't think you need to worry. I should say the risk is certainly greater in that direction, if we're talking in terms of someone diddling someone else. The difference lies mostly in that we wouldn't show such bad taste as to imply any such thing."

"Oh, there's nothing wrong with money," said Charlotte. "And we'll make sure we look after our own interests, won't we, John?"

"Yes, Fredrik saw to that, I think."

"We've borrowed nothing, for instance. Now it looks as if the whole family had gone to her to borrow money. How can that be fair? If Dad had been able to borrow in the same way, he could have had his own business by now, perhaps years ago. Account has to be taken of that kind of thing, doesn't it, John?"

John nodded reluctantly. His pale, narrow face did not indicate great sources of energy or willpower, so Ellen was surprised when he turned roughly toward her and said arrogantly, almost menacingly, "I want to make it clear to any of you who don't have your affairs in order in this business. If there's anything to find out, then it'll have to be brought into the open. I'd be glad to act on behalf of Fredrik. I could watch over his interests, since I've been an accountant for quite some time, and I'm capable of auditing accounts and balance sheets."

"Goodness me," said Victor with simulated terror. "So you're going to watch over Fredrik's interests, are you? Not your own or Charlotte's? Have you thought that perhaps Fredrik might cheat even you?"

"Nonsense!" John's face clouded and for a moment he looked confused. Charlotte laughed shrilly.

"John, have you ever been anything else but Fredrik's errand boy?" Victor went on. "I think you damned well married Charlotte just because Fredrik told you to. You're pushed around, John. Just like Ulla. Just as he tries to push us all around. You're pushed around from all directions, father-in-law and mother-in-law and wife and debit and credit and profit and loss. What about thinking for yourself, for a change, taking yourself by the scruff of the neck and having opinions of your own and watching over your *own* interests. Look at *her*." He thrust his forefinger into Charlotte's side. "She's been a dependent goose all her life. Terrified of Daddy, and worried about Mommy, always doing and thinking what they've wanted her to. But you—you let yourself be pushed around by *her*, too. Audit accounts—for Christ's sake. What if it turns out they're all in order and they've been trying to tell you they're not? And what if they're not in order and they've wanted you to believe they are? I think you should stop implying something is fishy when you don't have the foggiest damn idea of the whole situation. That goes for you, too, Charlotte. And for Fredrik and for Ulla and for the whole damned shitty family."

Victor had talked himself red in the face. Ellen glanced over at Ulla and saw that she was just as alarmed, perhaps even more so, since she probably didn't know that this was how Victor usually reacted when he lost his temper. Charlotte got up, as red in the face as Victor. She mumbled something about having to see to little Charlene and walked over to the kitchen corridor. Then Victor's anger dissolved as suddenly as it had come, and his face lit up with a charmer's smile, which she was at once able to diagnose. The next moment she heard Malin's slow, breathy voice saying, "Shall we dance, Victor?"

As he got up from the sofa and escorted her toward the music with one hand on her hip, Ellen also got up and went to the upper hall to escape from these hostile, meaningless discussions.

Ellen emerged from her thoughts just as Vera swung onto the road leading to the manor.

"What do you think of Malin?" Ellen said.

"She's all right. She certainly has an effect."

Vera looked at her. "I could see you didn't like her dancing with Martin—in that way—but that was probably effective, that too—poor Martin."

"What does she do? Wasn't she a stewardess?"

"Ellen, dear, that was ages ago. She works for Mauritz now
—secretarial work, that kind of thing. Victor looked interested, too, didn't he? Rather taken, if you know what I mean."

"Yes, I know what you mean. Martin and Victor had the
same taste. I was just wondering . . ."

Ellen didn't really know what she had been wondering.

They drove up the avenue of birches that ended at the
front of the house. Vera swung the car around, stopped just
by the veranda, and turned off the ignition.

"There we are," she said. "I'll wait here while you check
the machine."

All was well in the hen house. Out of habit, Ellen felt for
eggs in the boxes, and found herself wondering whether she
should take a basket back to Aunt Lethander this time as
well, but the thought was, of course, absurd. Then she went
to the stables and saw that the horses had just been fed. That
calmed her. The Werner boys were not there, but they had
done what they should have. She went back to the car.

"I'll just go in and get a raincoat," she said. "It's cloud-
ing over."

She went up the veranda steps, took out her keys, and
unlocked the door. As soon as she opened the door she had a
strange feeling that something had happened in the house
since she had last been there. She looked around the rooms,
but everything seemed normal. She finally opened the door
of Martin's study and went in to look around. Everything was
in order there, too, but then she suddenly saw his keys. For a
while she stared at them in bewilderment, then she picked
them up and put them in her bag, her sense of uncertainty
increasing. Was it possible? As long as she could remember he
had never done that before—not even when changing suits, or

in a hurry, or simply absentmindedly. It was a reflex for him to carry his keys on him, always.

When she went out, she said to Vera, "I don't understand. Martin did something yesterday I'm certain he'd never done before."

"What?"

"He forgot his keys on his desk. That's why they weren't found on him."

Vera made no comment until Ellen was in the car again and they were on their way back. Then she said in passing, "You know, I think that'd interest the police. He didn't necessarily forget the keys. Perhaps he *had* them on him, but someone took them, perhaps because someone needed them, perhaps because someone was going to come here. Then someone drove here. Then it's possible someone forgot them here or wanted it to look as if Martin had forgotten them."

Ellen felt her confusion increasing, and as if to clarify her thoughts, she said, "What was it you wanted to talk to me about yesterday?"

Vera glanced over at her. "What d'you mean?"

"When you called. When I was in the hen house. Martin answered the phone."

"I didn't call. Where did you get that idea from?"

"Martin was talking on the phone. I saw him myself. He said you'd called. In the afternoon, before we went back. Between four and five."

Vera did not reply. For a long stretch she drove in silence, the soft, humming noise of the engine making a pleasing, calming sound. Then she broke the silence. "If anyone took the keys, one must ask *why* anyone would want them, and *what* anyone would want them *for*. Tell me, Ellen—which of the family brought cars with them?"

Ellen obediently thought about it.

"Victor and you girls came in his car," she said. "The Svenssons came by bus from Stockholm to Gislaved, then took a taxi out to the house. Malin has a car. Mauritz came by car, but that wasn't until this morning. Then there's Aunt Lethander's old Volvo. I don't know of any others."

"I do," said Vera. "This one. I don't know if you noticed it, but the doors were unlocked when we got in. And the key was in the ignition. Wouldn't it be logical for someone to use this particular car, since of course it was just as easy to take the car keys as the key ring from Martin? Or be *given* them? Just which is hard to say."

11

DURELL

DURELL PACED BACK AND FORTH ACROSS THE KITCHEN FLOOR, unconsciously adapting his steps to the squares in the linoleum and stepping only on the blue ones, avoiding the well-scrubbed cleanliness of the white ones. The kitchen table was large and circular, dominating the window wall. John and Charlotte Bokström were sitting at it, both clearly nervous. The accountant was fidgeting, his hands shifting about on the tabletop, as if sweeping away invisible crumbs or scraping with his nails at an invisible spot on the spotless surface. He had a short, thin reddish beard, which Durell thought made a good contrast with his hunting-green lumber jacket. But the lumber jacket was not the most suitable garment for this man, whose face was far too thin and pale, his shoulders too sloping and narrow. An ordinary jacket would have suited him much better. But the color scheme was excellent. His wife looked old for her age, about thirty-five, Durell reckoned, plump, filling up her blouse and skirt a little too well, her flesh beginning to lose its tautness, and her double chin looking larger than it really was. She was also nervous, sitting rigidly upright, her hands in her lap. He couldn't see directly, since the table was in the way, but from the movement of her shoulders and upper arms he guessed she was continuously twisting her hands.

Durell had asked them to come because one of the younger men, Carl, brother of Charlotte Bokström, had hinted that the two of them had something to tell him about the shot.

He cleared his throat.

"Let's go back to the beginning again, shall we?" he said. "The party was over and you were sitting alone in the library, watching the lightning."

"Yes, that's right," said Charlotte. "We were sitting there holding hands, trying to forget what a terrible failure the whole party had been."

"You mean the exchange between your father and Miss Lethander?"

"Yes, of course. It was really dreadful. But not just that . . . we had a fight with Martin, too. And Victor. We couldn't possibly have known *then* what was going to happen, because it hadn't happened yet—the quarrel, I mean. And then everything was spoiled. We kept to ourselves, and the others kept to themselves, and then they started dancing, of course—"

John interrupted her. "We don't like dancing very much. You grow out of that sort of thing, don't you? It was nothing but a lot of flirting and silliness, making everyone angry with everyone else in some way."

"I see," said Durell. "Your sister-in-law . . ."

"No, not just her," said Charlotte. "They were all the same. Charles and Malin, and the Bernheim girls and Victor. Victor's red shirt was like a magnet. Like a flame to a moth, as Vera said. Both Gittan and Malin. Or course, the boys got furious. Both Charles and that Yugoslav, though he didn't show much. Anyhow, he left so early, you knew what he thought."

"But Charles showed he was furious, didn't he?" said Durell, as innocently as possible, and unsuspectingly Charlotte gave him the answer.

"They almost started fighting here in the kitchen at one point, but Charles calmed down. Then they disappeared. We didn't see either of them, as far as I can remember, until the house was quiet again and everyone had gone to bed. Gittan came into the library, where John and I were watching the lightning."

"Holding hands?"

"Yes."

Durell paused, figuring he had now established the prelude to it all.

"And so you went on sitting there by the window until midnight?" he said.

"Roughly, yes," replied John. "I have a habit of looking at my watch when something moves into a new phase, so to speak. When I go to bed, for instance, or get up. Or when I go to lunch, or the telephone rings, or something like that. It's a useful habit because then you know exactly when things happen. We went to our room at four minutes past midnight."

"You know that for certain."

"Yes."

"And you're certain your watch is accurate?"

John Bokström made a smug face and simply nodded in reply.

"At this time the house was quiet and peaceful?"

"Yes, it was," said Charlotte. "Aside from the fact that our little girl woke up when we came in and started crying a little. Otherwise she was as quiet as a mouse all evening, despite all the noise and quarreling in the house. Then she went to sleep again and we went to bed."

"And then?"

"We went to sleep, of course. At first John . . . John tried . . . but I didn't want to, partly because I was tired, and partly because he smelled of booze, and I was so irritated by all that messing around, so I just said I wanted to sleep. And . . . well, then I fell asleep."

"And you, Mr. Bokström? You looked at your watch?"

He sniffed, and Durell also noticed that he actually turned slightly red.

"Yes, I did. It was half past twelve by then."

"So now we come to the interesting part, Mrs. Bokström. You said you woke up again."

Charlotte drew another deep breath. "Yes. The car woke me. A car engine started somewhere down in the front, and I probably wouldn't have woken up if Charlene hadn't started crying again—only a little cry but enough to wake me. I always wake as soon as she makes a sound—we mothers are often like that. I got up and went over to her, but she had already fallen asleep again by then. Then I went and looked out the window, which faces out to the front, and I caught sight of a car disappearing toward the road. Not only that"— she paused dramatically—"it had only its parking lights on."

"And what time was it then?" asked Durell hopefully.

She shook her head. "I don't know. I'm not like John, always looking at the time. But I couldn't go back to sleep. I lay there for what seemed like ages, thinking about things and, you know, everything that had happened that evening, and it went around and around in my head, as it does when you can't sleep. Then I lay listening to John's breathing, and Charlene's. I don't know how long. And then the car came back."

"Oh, yes, then the car came back. Can you estimate how long it had been away?"

"It's awfully difficult because even if you can't sleep, you sort of *half* sleep in between. You have no real idea of time."

"But roughly?"

She gazed around the kitchen, her eyes wide open and uncertain, then she pouted and said hesitantly, "An hour, maybe. Maybe less, maybe a little more."

"And you didn't get up to look that time?"

"No. There was no reason to, either, because I didn't think it was anything special. At least, not then."

"Even though the car had driven away with the lights off?"

Durell sounded almost reproachful. She did not reply but made an unhappy little gesture with her hands, which now lay on the table.

"And then there was the shot?" Durell went on.

"Yes. Then there was the shot. I can't tell you exactly where it came from because none of us knew then what we know now, but . . . I mean . . . I was still awake but probably just falling asleep when there was a shot. It was just like with the car—our little girl woke up and started crying again, so I was wide awake at once, of course. This time I wasn't the only one to wake. John did, too. 'What was that?' he said. 'What was that bang? Can't you get the kid to be quiet?' I thought that was awfully unfair of him because she'd already stopped crying. Well, I was already up by then, and since I'd thought the bang had come from just outside the window, I looked out again, of course. But there was nothing there. I saw nothing whatsoever out there."

"Nothing? You said . . . ?" Durell looked at her.

"Yes, there was a light on in the wing, of course. Where Malin and the Yugoslav were. And I saw Malin moving about inside the room. I thought they'd also heard the shot and had got up to see what the sound was. But when I asked her about it earlier today, when we were having tea this morning in the kitchen, after that terrible discovery and everyone had to make do for themselves and Alma was walking around looking stunned and she was *also* talking about hearing the shot, then Malin maintained she hadn't heard a thing. She was just going to . . . I don't know what it was she said she was just going to do. But *I* heard the shot, anyhow, and so did John, and so did Alma, and the shot was just above us."

Durell looked thoughtfully at her. Then he said suddenly, "Did you notice whether there was a light on in the Rosceffs' room the first time you got up? I mean, when you heard the car?"

"It was dark there then," said Charlotte firmly. "If there'd been a light on, I'm sure I'd have noticed. It was dark everywhere, but this time there were lights on in half the windows. And then—the first time—it was just because it *was* so dark everywhere that I especially noticed the car driving with only its parking lights on."

"Tell me, Mrs. Bokström, had the thunder stopped by then? I mean, you couldn't possibly have mistaken the thunder for a shot, could you?"

Charlotte looked offended.

"No," she said curtly. "The thunder had stopped. The thunder had ended by the time we went to bed, John and I. And anyhow, I'd never mix up the sound of a shot with an ordinary clap of thunder."

"I'm sure you wouldn't. So it was the shot you heard. The shot that meant the end of Victor Bernheim."

Charlotte was now looking very confident and self-satisfied.

"Yes, I think I can say that."

"And when was that, did you say?"

Durell turned to John, who also had that look of self-satisfaction that indisputable knowledge produces.

"It was *exactly* twenty past two. *Exactly*, I said."

Durell gazed at them. There was no doubt they knew what they were talking about, and he was convinced all this could be written in his report. On the other hand, one of the statements had confused him and made him hesitate.

"Would you be kind enough," he said benignly to Charlotte, "to ask Miss Lethander's housekeeper to come here? As you said, she also heard the shot, which isn't all that surprising, since her room is next to yours. But—well—it might be interesting to hear *her* version."

Charlotte got up awkwardly and left the kitchen. John Bokström and Durell waited in silence. Then Charlotte returned with Alma, thickset and dignified, as white-haired as Miss Lethander but at least thirty years younger, wearing a blue dress and spotless white apron. She remained standing as she looked at Durell, who was still standing on the blue squares of linoleum. Charlotte went back to the wooden bench by the kitchen table and sat down next to her husband.

"Miss Gren, I understand you heard the shot last night."

"Yes, Inspector, I did."

"Mr. and Mrs. Bokström did, too."

"Yes, they told me this morning. Their room is almost directly below that room, although mine is nearer. It was horrible to hear, Inspector. At the time, of course, I didn't realize just *how* horrible."

"You looked automatically at the time, is that right?"

"Automatically . . ." She hesitated. "I got up and looked, of course. I got up and looked out the window because I wasn't sure where it had come from."

"Did you also think it might have come from outside?"

"No, not at all. I heard clearly that it came from upstairs. From Victor's room. But I wanted to find out, all the same."

"Was it a very loud shout?"

She looked uncertain again. "Well, it was loud, yes. It was a shot."

"But not *terribly* loud."

"Quite loud . . ." She looked appealingly at Charlotte, who nodded in agreement.

"You must remember," Alma went on, "that it came from above. It wouldn't sound as it would have in the same room, you know."

"No, of course not. I see that," Durell agreed. "And *when* was it you heard this shot?"

"Exactly one o'clock."

"One o'clock." Durell smiled mysteriously, at the same time noting Charlotte's and John's confusion. "You're absolutely certain about that?"

"Absolutely."

Alma walked firmly past Durell and pointed at the kitchen clock on the wall between the refrigerator and the pantry in the corner. Durell followed her.

"When I heard the shot," Alma went on, "I came straight here into the kitchen to get a glass of milk, and I looked at the clock, which said exactly one o'clock."

Suddenly her confidence faded, the expression on her face changing to one of confusion.

"Good gracious," she said, almost to herself. "It says one

o'clock *now*. Could . . . could it have stopped? Could I really have made such a mistake?"

As if doubting herself, she went right up to the clock and listened.

"Yes, it's stopped," she said, still confused. "Then I must have . . . then I don't really know . . . I'm terribly sorry . . ."

Durell smiled cheerfully at her.

"Don't worry about that," he said. "We know when the shot occurred. Mr. and Mrs. Bokström tell me it was at twenty past two. *Exactly* twenty past two. And we're equally grateful to have you as witness to the shot as we are to know that the actual time of it has been determined."

12

VERONICA

THE POLICE DIDN'T LEAVE THE HOUSE UNTIL ABOUT SEVEN, and most of us were greatly relieved when they went. But first they took all our fingerprints. No one special was suspected, but the assistant who took them had said, "We have to have prints of all the injured parties." Then he added, "You never can tell." He didn't explain what you could never tell. I asked what injured-party prints were and got a vague answer about their being "required" prints. So it was obvious they'd found fingerprints in Martin's or Victor's room, or perhaps in both. As far as "required" prints were concerned, I found it hard to understand that any prints other than Martin's or Victor's own, or possibly Alma's or even Aunt Lethander's, could be regarded as "required."

Not long after the cars had disappeared, Alma put a meal on the kitchen table, almost a repeat of the previous day's buffet, except that we all stayed in the kitchen. Malin and Sergej weren't there. Mauritz came in and asked Alma to arrange a tray for them, and said he would take it with him when he had finished. Alma protested firmly, saying there was no question about who should take it. She would. "In this house, guests are always treated as guests," she said. Ulla and Fredrik hadn't turned up, either, nor Ellen, who had said she couldn't eat a thing, but she had asked Vera and me if we would take a bottle of sherry with us if we could find any.

Vera helped herself liberally and took her plate with her over to Charles, a provocative look on her face.

"How's that lip of yours?" she said. "How did you get it, anyhow?"

Charles clenched his teeth and didn't reply.

"Too much running in the forest," Vera went on maliciously. "You must look where you're going, or you'll run into something."

Mauritz was standing there, smiling sourly. Carl took a sudden interest in what this might lead to and walked over to Charlotte, as if showing solidarity.

Vera looked at him with approval.

"Be like Carl instead," she said. "Calm, quiet, silent, and discreet. Carl is a gentleman, although he's a revolutionary down to his fingertips." She pointed at the little badge in his narrow lapel.

Mauritz's expression darkened. He put a small piece of bread into his mouth and said provocatively, "Why are you a member of the FNL, Carl?"

Carl smiled benignly. "So that it'll be legal when I slit your throat one fine day. Unfortunately, not all capitalists exterminate themselves." There was total silence, his unpleasant remark hanging in the air and filling the kitchen. Alma was the most disturbed. Carl went on. "But I may be too late—your daughter stands a good chance of being there first. But it's great the extermination process has started."

I turned icy cold at his words. I knew Carl was cynical—at least in his attitudes—but this was going too far. The only consolation was that Ellen wasn't there—she couldn't have coped with it—and Fredrik—because he would have laughed. I was sure Alma would tell Aunt Lethander about it, and that was also some consolation.

At that moment Ulla looked in through the door, wearing only a dressing gown, her hair gray and untidy around her ears. She looked as if she hadn't slept for several days. In the silence her flickering gaze settled on Carl.

"When I asked you for a headache pill yesterday," she whimpered, "did you take my sleeping pills? Fredrik denies he ever touched them, and all of them can't possibly have been used up. Carl, dear, have you hidden them from me?"

Carl seemed unsympathetic.

"Of course not," he said.

"No, of course not."

Ulla repeated his reply with a weary look, gazing around in the hope that someone else might help her. Then she said suddenly, "Where's Gittan?"

"She's asleep," said Charlotte.

Her reply surprised me. Not that Gittan would be asleep but that I hadn't noticed she wasn't there. Carl laughed.

"Gittan's asleep. I expect Charles gave her a couple of your sleeping pills to get her to sleep well last night."

Charles started as if bitten by a snake, and it was clear that the remark had been just as poisonous.

"Gittan doesn't take sleeping pills."

"Of course not. But perhaps you got a couple into her to stop her gadding about. Going to see someone else, I mean. Sergej, for instance. With someone as beautiful as she is, you never know where you are with her."

Or as dumb, I thought.

Charles put his plate down and leaned toward Carl with his fists clenched on his hips.

"What the hell d'you mean?"

"You know what I mean," said Carl dryly. "Not only do horns grow out of your forehead, but you also get a swollen lip. Hell, Charles, don't you think everyone noticed Victor and Gittan disappearing last night? And that you disappeared shortly afterward? Did you find them?"

"You *swine.*"

Charles bellowed out the word like a foghorn, his right fist simultaneously jabbing straight into Carl's solar plexus.

Carl doubled up like a jackknife, staggered back against a chair, and sank down in it, blue in the face, but managed to keep hold of the plate he had been holding out in front of him all the time.

"Boys, *stop* it, *stop* it . . ."

It was Alma's voice vibrating painfully in our ears. Vera and I had been listening to the quarrel with some amusement, Vera even quite expectantly, as if hoping for a fight. But there was no amusement in Alma's voice. It wasn't just a cry, but almost a scream of desperate appeal for them to stop. Neither time nor place nor state of mind was right for such arguments and quarrels and accusations. She said no more than that, no doubt because she couldn't have said more without bursting into tears. She picked up Malin's tray, which she had silently been arranging while she had been listening to the fight, and headed for the kitchen door.

Charles watched her go, letting her almost reach the door before he called her back. She turned around and looked at him.

"Alma," he said, "we've always managed to settle these little differences without interference before. You want to treat guests as guests, don't you, and talking to guests in that way is not done." He paused, looking straight at her, then went on. "What you do in the company of Miss Lethander is one thing, but this is another matter. Remember in the future. And remember, sometimes there are little birds listening in the forest."

Alma trembled but did not reply. I felt sorry for her and thought that Charles's behavior was abominable. I couldn't stop myself. I got up from the table and almost spat at Charles the only words I could think of at the moment. "Shame on you." Then I left the kitchen.

Ulla held the door open for Alma as she took the tray out, and she also kept it open for me. We went along the corridor and out into the hall. Ulla was walking slowly and thoughtfully. In the hall, she sat down on the sofa along the short wall. She hadn't said a word since we'd left the kitchen, and she seemed increasingly sunk in thought. I could hear voices rising and falling back in the kitchen, then, after a great burst of laughter, the door opened and someone came out. It was Charles. I could see from far away that he was white with rage.

"Poor Charles," said Ulla. "He's so hot-tempered. He's silly, too, to take it so hard. He gets that from his father."

She got up and I heard her mumble, "I must calm him down . . . and I must know what he meant . . ."

She stopped him a few strides away from me. He halted, though for a moment I thought he was going to knock her over.

"Charles," she said. "What did you mean in the kitchen— what you said to Alma? Birds in the forest, you said. And all that about what she did in Aunt Lethander's company?"

"What did I mean?" he snorted at her. "I meant that I heard Alma and Aunt Lethander quarreling loudly yesterday on their afternoon walk. I was out running, and happened to run the same way they were going. And although they didn't see me, I saw them, and I heard Alma shout just as loudly as she did just now in the kitchen. 'You can't do that,' she shrieked. 'I'll stop you at any price.' "

He looked at Ulla coldly. "Does that satisfy you?"

"Yes. You poor thing." She looked at him with pity. "Your lip—did you run into a tree?"

Charles closed his eyes and hissed, "Oh, shut up . . . I should have murdered the bastard . . ." Then he rushed through the hall toward his room and his waiting, possibly sleeping, beautiful wife.

I left Ulla, now seated on the sofa again, hoping that Vera wouldn't forget to bring that bottle of sherry with her.

It started to rain later that evening. Vera was lying on her bed, thoughtfully gazing at her fingertips; the ink from the fingerprinting procedure clearly annoyed her. Ellen was sitting on my bed with a glass of sherry in her hand. The bottle was almost empty. I had taken out my sketch pad. I usually took one with me on a trip, to jot down ideas for new clothes for my boutique. You never knew when inspiration would come, perhaps from the shape of a cloud, or a tree, or anything. I scratched the pen across the paper in the hope that it would produce some interesting lines I could work on. But it didn't.

Vera said suddenly, "Did you give the keys to the police?"

Ellen nodded. "Yes, I gave them to Melander."

"No comment? That little redhead, Durell, seems alert to me."

"They were going to drive over and take a look around," said Ellen. "They didn't seem as interested as you'd have thought. I'm glad I didn't have to go with them."

"Did you say anything about the car?"

"I told them someone might have used our car."

"Did you tell them where Martin had the pistol—in which drawer?"

"Yes. They asked me about that. They asked me lots of questions about the pistol, but I didn't even know he had one until the other day."

"Do you think Victor knew?"

"I have no idea. But I told him yesterday."

"You did?"

Vera suddenly lost interest in her fingertips and swung around on her side to lie with her head propped on her hand and her elbow on the pillow.

"I was worried," Ellen went on, "about Martin going around with that pistol on him, but I never thought he might use it against Victor. I didn't know anything about the . . ." She bit her lip, then drank the last drops in her glass.

"Blackmail," Vera finished for her.

"Yes."

"Did you tell Melander he had it *on* him?"

"I said something about things having gone so far that Martin was walking around with a pistol in his pocket."

I swiftly sketched a blouselike shape with a few extra contours below the bust, as if there were a pistol there, but then abandoned the idea.

Vera looked thoughtful. "Do you think anyone *else* knew he had a pistol on him?"

Ellen poured out some more sherry. "How would I know that?"

"No, of course not. I meant if someone else might have heard you when you were telling Victor. Or whether Martin had boasted about it. Or . . . anyhow, it's not certain he had it on him. He might have had it in his room. He was dancing, wasn't he? You can't dance with a pistol in your inside pocket. Your partner would feel it. Perhaps he had it in his suitcase or in a box . . ."

She sat up suddenly, then got up and went into the bathroom, leaving the door open. I heard her snort.

"What's wrong with this hairdo? I should have come back with something really nasty."

I put my pen down out of sheer surprise. Had she really been so offended by that remark made the day before, or rather the evening before, during the party? Gittan, Vera, Malin, and I happened to be together, and suddenly Gittan had placed her well-manicured hand with its long, shiny silver nails on Vera's arm and, blinking her eyelashes, had said, "Can't we be friends? You seem so disapproving when you look at me, as if you didn't like my being good-looking."

"Ah, my darling," Vera answered, taking off her glasses. "We've never been exactly passionate esthetes in our family, with the possible exception of Veronica. So you're good-looking."

"Don't you think so?"

Vera was noticeably irritated. "What are you getting at?" she snapped.

"You're jealous because I'm better-looking than you, and

that's why you're so unfriendly. Your brother said you didn't think much of me."

"Indeed? I don't think I've said anything about you to my brother."

"I like your brother," said Gittan, smiling with her mouth half open. "He's the kind of man I fall for. Charles is, too, but then I've got him already."

Vera turned away and Malin started laughing quietly. Gittan noticed and at once turned to her instead. "Your man isn't bad, either, but I'm tired of that black-mustache type. They're all over the place in Majorca—I don't know *how* many men like that I've been with. They love my type. But you're really far too tall for him." She tittered coquettishly. Malin appeared unmoved, but I noticed Vera was boiling with rage. Gittan went on chattering, offering her opinions of herself and various men and how she could choose and discard and take her pick here and there and that she had a good but particular appetite when it came to consuming men. Then she went on to how life was mostly loving and having fun, glancing across at Victor, who was over by the radio looking for a suitable dance tune, his red shirt like blood in the light from the lamp. "Enjoy the wide spectrum of love as in a dance over the rainbow," she declaimed. No, she said, she hadn't made that up. Someone had whispered it in her ear after a rain shower.

"Imagine that," said Vera sarcastically. "I've always thought the spectrum of love in the Svensson family depressingly narrow. Before you appeared on the scene, there was only the love of money. So now that's been complemented—with self-love."

Gittan's eyes widened and she stared in surprise and incomprehension.

"Money," she said. "I don't care for money at all."

"I was trying to make a generalization," said Vera curtly. "But I realize profundities are not exactly your line."

"Now you're being nasty," said Gittan. "I can't help looking as I do. Or that men like it. Why should I have to be profound, if that's what you mean?" Then she said it. "Anyhow, I wouldn't have my hair cut short if I were you and had that shape face and broad chin. And those awful glasses."

Vera's face clouded.

"Malin's is much nicer," Gittan went on, smiling innocently. "I expect that's because she's got someone she likes to make herself nice for."

She suddenly looked suspiciously at Vera. "Perhaps you don't like men?"

"Why shouldn't I like men?"

"You're too smart. You're involved in politics and that sort of thing. Carl told me that. He likes you, even though you're one of those horrible capitalists. He doesn't like Victor at all. Or your father."

Vera moistened her lips. "Neither do I. It's just possible that those two examples have made me slightly more cautious than you when it comes to men."

"Is that why you have your hair cut like that?" She looked at Vera with her head to one side. "I must say I think your father's dishy. I find older men difficult. They always want to talk so much . . ." She stopped and a soft shadow flitted across her lovely face. Then she went on. "Carl doesn't believe in God. Do you know why?"

"You've got a clever brother-in-law," said Vera acidly. "It's lucky we've got him in the family, so we don't have to look elsewhere. *Your* contribution is as light as a feather."

"What do you mean?" said Gittan, her blue eyes blank.

"I was thinking of the family intelligence. It's almost cruel of Charles to dilute it even more by choosing you as a discussion partner for life."

"Discussion partner?" Her lower lip trembled slightly as she went on. "We don't usually discuss anything. I don't know what you mean . . . but . . . I think you're being nasty, and when people are nasty to me, I'm miserable . . . miserable, don't you see?"

I figured it was high time to cut in, and in a much too loud voice, which made Victor turn around and consider coming over to us, I said, "Leave her alone now."

"Yes, of course," said Vera. "If you're dumb, you're dumb, aren't you?"

But Gittan's lower lip went on trembling and she cried out, "I don't have to put up with this. I'll show you—you can bet I will."

Vera burst out laughing and Malin turned her back on us all. Gittan ran across to Victor and I saw them talking to each other, quietly and intently.

"Girls like that are death to men," said Vera icily.

I felt depressed at the thought of this interlude, which in fact I'd forgotten as soon as it was over. But Vera had taken it badly. I saw her through the doorway, leaning forward and examining her face very thoroughly, holding her hands around her hair and trying to get it to look longer and fuller. Then she gave up and started rubbing soap into her finger-tips and scrubbing them with the nail brush. But she gave that up, too, and came out again.

"I must get rid of this mess," she said. "I'll go see if Alma has any strong detergent." She threw Ellen's raincoat over her shoulders and set off in the darkness, the door slamming behind her with a bang. I was feeling despondent. Some worthless sketches were lying on the table, and I picked up my pen and drew crisscross lines over them.

"Give me some inspiration," I said. "For heaven's sake, Ellen, help me get something done."

Ellen sipped from her glass and thought, then said, "There must be lots of amusing old clothes in Aunt Lethander's attic. Perhaps you can find something there?"

The idea interested me at once. Why on earth hadn't I thought of it before? There must be plenty of nineteenth-century ideas up there that would be just right for me. I flung down my pen and got up. Ellen looked at me in surprise.

"Are you going right now?"

"Can't wait," I said. "I *must* go see what's there."

I didn't even bother to find anything to cover my hair, but ran across to the house. I should have worn a hat because it was raining hard, the rain glittering and glistening in the lights from indoors. There were lights on in both wings and the windows were warm yellow rectangles.

But the main part of the house was dark, not a single light in any of the windows, and although I didn't give it much thought I was somewhat surprised that everyone had already gone to bed. Well, I suppose they all needed sleep after such a trying day, and it was after eleven.

I closed the front door behind me and fumbled around in the dark for the switch. The light from the chandelier almost blinded me. I stood still listening for a few moments and the whole house was completely quiet. So quiet I unconsciously started tiptoeing upstairs to the second floor, since I was afraid my footsteps might echo throughout the house. I switched on the light upstairs and turned out the downstairs light. I went through the dining room, along the corridor to Aunt Lethander's apartment, almost to the end, still tiptoeing so I wouldn't wake the old lady.

The door to the attic was slightly ajar, which was a relief, because I knew it squeaked. I fumbled along the wall until I found the switch and turned it on. A feeble light spread over the stairs twisting upward in a steep half spiral, a thin wooden railing on one side. As quietly as I could, I climbed the stairs, pleased they didn't creak. I hardly dared breathe naturally because I had an unfounded sense of being out on a forbidden mission, like a thief in the night, and I was beginning to regret not having postponed this expedition until the following day. But then I would have lost my inspiration.

At last I was in the attic, which was directly beneath the roof of the house, the floors of boards from hundred-year-old spruces, wide and strong at one end, then slowly narrowing until they spliced into others, making a sparse, irregular pattern of transverse lines, like a giant parquet floor. High up above was the roof construction, its beams and rafters dim in the half-light. I could see only a faint outline of everything, mysterious spaces and corners fading away into nothing, and beams looking as if they were floating.

The attic wardrobes were in a row along one wall, underneath square skylights of dusty glass, through the slats looking like patches of mist in the darkness. I started having doubts. Was it too dark up here? Would I find anything useful? I went across to the dressing room, where I saw to my relief a naked bulb hanging from the ceiling, and for the third time I fumbled for the switch inside the slatted door. I switched it on. Nothing happened. Typical of my bad luck that the bulb was dead. I looked around inside the dressing room, my eyes now beginning to get used to the half-light, and found I could see well enough to be able to pick out what seemed interesting. I could look at things more closely in the corner room.

The dressing room was large. On the left were rows of garments on hangers, mostly from the end of the 1800s and the following decades—long frockcoats and crinolines that had probably been worn by Aunt Lethander's parents, embroidered blouses, silk shawls, old feather boas and dusty plumes, a pale blue lace dress from the twenties shimmering like sapphire in the dim light, and alongside it a long fur coat I would have liked to show in my boutique window. That was all I could immediately identify. But there were lots of other clothes—dresses, skirts, blouses. It was like finding a treasure trove. There were rows of old footwear lined up beneath the clothes, low shoes, boots, hand-sewn ankle boots with high heels and long laces, shoes my ancestors had no doubt worn and that would still remind old Aunt Lethander of happy parties in the days when she was the young mistress. They were striped with shadows from the slats, which suddenly reminded me of prison bars. Opposite the clothes was an old open cabinet containing rows of office files, account books, and newspaper clippings. The dust had settled in patches, and I could see spiderwebs in the corners, some of them torn away and trailing ghostlike down the shelves. The whole place gave me a creepy feeling of increasing unreality.

I put a few dresses across my arm and went out and over to the corner room. It was an exciting room. One wall was semicircular with an oriel window, deep inside which was a narrow window with small square panes and yellow cotton curtains. They glowed like amber when the sun shone through them. As a child I had loved sleeping in this room and waking in the morning, lying in the old iron bed looking out toward the light and daydreaming. Then, when I got up, I used to pad between the rag rugs, where the floor was bare and scrubbed smooth, like walking on velvet as I went over to the washstand and the heavy flowered china washbasin and jug. I remembered what it was like at night when it was raining, as it was tonight, listening to the patter against the copper roofing capping the tower. I was never frightened of sleeping there, although the room was isolated from the rest of the house, and the desolate attic outside with its single light bulb hanging from a beam was tailormade for stories with sighing ghosts and creaking footsteps. Alongside the oriel window was a desk with brass handles on the drawers and a rickety monk's seat in front of it, a brown leather armchair and a butler's tray on the other side. Opposite the iron bedstead, the wall was taken up with a heavy wardrobe and alongside that was the washstand.

I put the garments down on the bed and examined them carefully. Some of the amusing pleats at the hips might be of use in the future, but at the moment they weren't worth copying. All these clothes should be left for a few more years. I went back to the dressing room and hung them up properly. If only the light had been better. I looked around and saw a wooden box alongside the file cabinet. Maybe—maybe the bulb was all right and just needed tightening. I pulled out the box, got up, and felt the bulb. It was, in fact, loose. I tightened it, but then a nasty sensation started rising in me. The bulb was loose, but there was something else. It was *warm*. I panicked. I thought of all those times Ellen, and Martin, too, for that matter, had come into our room when we were young and discovered we had ignored their orders to put the light out and go to sleep at once. They had always felt the bedside light bulbs.

I was paralyzed, standing on that box, too weak to get down from it. There was someone up here. Someone had been up here all the time. I tried to think coolly, gazing around, and then I made another discovery. A black hole was gaping in the row of shoes. In a kind of fog I realized that when I had first come in here, someone had been standing hidden behind the clothes. I had seen his shoes but had not understood. Now, when I tried to remember what kind of shoes were missing, I couldn't—I could only register the fact that a pair of shoes were missing, that there hadn't been a gap in the row before, but pair after pair in an unbroken line. Eventually my capacity to act started to come back. I got down from the box and pushed it back, trying to appear unconcerned. I went over to the switch and turned it on, filling the whole room with calming light. What should I do now? I thought feverishly. When I had come up or, rather, when *someone* had heard me coming up, he must have been in the dressing room with the light on. There had been no lights on in the rest of the attic. I knew I had turned on the lights, which meant someone must have crept up in the dark. Then—when he heard me on the stairs—he had unscrewed the bulb in the dressing room and hidden behind the clothes.

I thought hard. I had turned the switch in the dressing room *once*, just once. That meant I had in fact switched off the current. That was right—because the light hadn't gone on when I'd tightened the bulb. I had had to switch it on. But the big question was, was someone still up here? I couldn't be sure. He could have left when I was in the corner room. And the next question, What had he been doing up here?

And the next, Who was he? And the next, What should I do now? He might still be there. Perhaps he hadn't had time to finish his errand before I had disturbed him? Perhaps he still wanted to finish it?

I decided to keep cool and act as if I hadn't noticed anything. In a trance, I picked up a few more dresses and walked stiffly back to the corner room, leaving the door to the attic wide open. *If* the other person tried to get away unseen, it wouldn't work because I could see the top of the stairs. Then suddenly it happened. The light went out. All the lights went out. I screamed, threw down the dresses, and rushed out through the black door, into the black darkness outside, and fumbled along the wall to escape anything out there, filled with terror. As I fumbled my way forward I heard footsteps behind me, and in a moment of clarity in all that confusion I remembered a little fuse box just beyond the corner room, and I realized that whoever it was had taken out a fuse, and he had been there all the time—was now out there in the dark—and I . . .

Suddenly a beam of light shone out behind me like a flame. I pressed back against the wall and turned toward the light. The powerful cone of light from a flashlight shone straight into my eyes and blinded me completely. I wanted to scream but couldn't get a sound out, only suppressed little grunts as the steps came nearer, and I heard him panting. The blinding light glided past me in a semicircle without leaving my face for a single moment, then moved on toward the stairs, still straight in my eyes as I stood there, numbed and paralyzed. Then it dropped, flared up again, and vanished.

My paralysis released its stranglehold and I started screaming. I fumbled, stumbled, and crawled along the wall, got up again, and at last reached the stairs, screaming all the time, crying hysterically. On my way down I didn't know whether I would land in the arms of this unknown person, or whether I'd be able to get out, or whether I'd trip and hurtle down, smashing myself to pieces. At last I reached the bottom. The door was shut, locked from the outside. I started banging on it wildly, like a madman, my fists drumming loudly and numbly on the door. Finally the door opened. I collapsed like a rag.

It was light, a wonderful balm. My terror left me in a great warm wave. I looked up—Aunt Lethander's eyes. She was fully dressed and looking anxiously at me.

"Now, now, child. What's happened now?"

"Call the police."

"But no damage has been done. It's all right now, my child."

"No, no . . . it's not . . ."

I couldn't do anything but sob. Then I felt my heart thump as I saw what Aunt Lethander had in her hand. I pointed to it and managed to say, "What's . . . what's that?"

"My dear child," she said, smiling almost pityingly, "you can see perfectly well what it is. A flashlight."

13

DURELL

THE RINGING OF THE TELEPHONE SLOWLY PENETRATED THROUGH to Durell. With a reflex action, he turned over, fumbled around the bedside table, almost knocking over a glass, finally realizing he would have to get up to answer. Halfway between waking and sleep, he managed to remove the covers and get to his feet. He sat down at the desk. As he grabbed the telephone to reply he gazed thoughtfully at his toes.

"G'morning, Inspector," he heard in his ear. "It's six-thirty."

"Did you say six-thirty?"

"Yes, six-thirty."

Six-thirty, he thought, replacing the receiver. That meant he had had about four hours' sleep. Down deep he felt sorry for himself for having chosen such an uncomfortable life as a policeman's. He yawned, stretched, tried a fairly easy note, and thought it didn't sound too bad. He tried another, then another, then swept up and down the whole scale, first in one octave, then in the next, and finally in the three and a half that he could master.

It had been late last night. After the spadework at the old house had been done, the unfortunate Mrs. Bernheim had entrusted them with the bunch of keys they had not found on her husband. Melander and an assistant had taken them over to the manor to see whether that would produce anything. He himself had gone to the police station in Gislaved. There had been a number of things to be delegated. Some specific questions to the Stockholm crime division concerning Victor Bernheim and his circle of acquaintances. Some technical questions and technical checking—fingerprint analyses, examination of articles, and so on, which a courier had had to take to Jönköping. Inquiries about Mauritz Corn and his deceased wife and several other matters. Administering all this had not been easy. Nothing worse than a weekend murder, he thought. You want to talk to people, and they're inaccessible. You want information from the authorities, but they don't have access to the records on the weekend. You want to speak to a specialist. He says he will be back on Monday. Durell tried to recall whether he had ever been involved in a murder that had been solved on a Sunday. Alas, he hadn't. He sighed heavily, but not without satisfaction, because however troublesome it had been, much had been achieved, and many promises had already been made relating to a number of instructions.

When he finally sat down in the peace and quiet of his hotel room, he took out his Wendell directory and allowed that wise book to tell him everything it knew about carbon monoxide. And then, when he had gone to bed, his thoughts began to flow freely, flowing and dipping and searching and burrowing, rummaging around in the facts found and impressions gained during the day.

He got up and went over to the long wardrobe mirror. He did a few careful, swift knee bends, noting at the same time that hotel mirrors were nearly always made so that guests were happy to look in them. Even on a Monday morning.

He walked to the police station, where he found the news had spread. A couple of local press cars were parked outside, and as he went in he collided with a sleepy photographer on his way out, followed by a journalist still taking notes.

The latter recognized Durell and fired off the inevitable question, "Anything new on the murder?"

"No," said Durell, shaking his head.

"No one detained—no suspect?"

"No, no one detained and no suspect."

He let them pass and went into the red-brick police station to Melander's office, a long way from the cells. Melander disliked hearing the shouts and curses of drunks and trouble-makers, as he put it.

Melander was in the process of filling his first pipe of the day in order—as he said—to keep the pleasantly cozy aroma of tobacco in the walls and curtains. He had a notepad in front of him. Durell hoped the jottings he could see from his place opposite were going to be the first solid bricks of the case.

He nodded at the pad. "Got anything there?"

"A little. They've been at it all night. Let's take the ash first. We won't get the final analysis until Tuesday, but they've given us a provisional one. The fire was of birchwood."

"Really?" said Durell ironically. "They found that out, did they?"

Melander went on, unmoved. "There were also remains of burned paper, not just newspaper, but paper with writing on it. It might, for instance, have been a letter—but the fragments were small and carbonized, so they were impossible to piece together. Still, they've found some bits of writing through infrared photography. One says . . . *vil in my li* . . . Another says . . . *er the pre* . . . And lastly . . . *it you and your* . . ."

Melander paused for a moment before continuing. "You know," he said, "*two* of those fragments weren't in the fire-place at all, but *outside* it, on the floor."

"Uh-huh."

Durell pondered for a moment. "Are they typed?"

"No, ball point or ink. They'll find out which."

"And aside from that, it was all burned up?"

"Yes, all burned."

There was another pause.

"So it could have been the letter," said Durell. "I was thinking about the blackmail. Could this have been the letter about Stella? The one Martin was given, or took, or stole and burned in the fire?"

"Could be."

"But it could also be something completely different. It doesn't have to be a letter."

"No, of course not. It could be any kind of note."

"But not just *any* old note. It sounds too personal. 'You and your.' That implies a message of some kind, doesn't it? Or a letter."

"Yes, that's what I'm saying. It's *addressed* to someone. Someone has received it. Or had received it."

Durell pondered again.

"What did you say?" he went on. "*. . . vil in my li . . .* and then *. . . er the pre . . .* and last of all *. . . it you and your . . .* Is that right?"

"Exactly."

Durell straightened up and looked at Melander as if he were a crystal ball.

"Listen to me. 'There is a devil in my liver and I disown the preacher who tried to exorcise it. I would rather spirit you and your ridiculous advice to hell.' Or, 'The devil in my liver goes down the prescribed routes so there is no merit in you and your absurd cures.' Or . . .'"

Melander laughed. Looking solemnly at him, Durell said, "You see? It doesn't matter what your profession is. Now, then—handwritten, you say? Is the handwriting identifiable?"

"Don't know."

"Ask them to send copies of what they've got. And then take samples to the handwriting expert at HQ, and we'll see if he can find anything. If we get a bite, then maybe we can write this week's horoscope."

He laughed, his small fat fingers drumming on the desk. "That's that. Have you got anything else?"

"Burned rubber."

"Uh-huh. Almost to be expected. Was there some burned string, too?"

Melander's eyes widened. "Yes. How the hell did you know that?"

"Remember," said Durell demurely, "They had a *party* that night. They danced a balloon dance, which entails tying balloons around your legs and exposing yourself to assaults by all the other dancers while you also try to stamp on as many of the other balloons as possible to burst them. Wasn't that it? Yes, it was. Martin was also very much involved in that dance. The old rake. What could be more natural than to remove the remains when you go to bed and throw them in the fire?"

"By all means," said Melander. "Do you *know* that he joined in the balloon dance?"

"They say so," said Durell, chuckling. "And if he didn't, then it was someone else."

"Supposing it was a condom? The old rake . . ."

Durell looked at him skeptically. "With string around it? No, I prefer the balloon theory."

Melander refused to be put off. "You said perhaps it was someone else. Then it must have been someone who was in Martin's room that evening."

"Oh, yes. But not necessarily at the same time."

"Do people usually throw popped balloons into fires? They smell. Wouldn't a wastepaper basket be more suitable?"

"Yes, of course. Tell the person who did it. In this case the rubbish *was* actually thrown in the fire."

Melander started laughing again, then leaned back in his revolving chair, his long figure shaking with silent chuckles. He stopped suddenly and said, "Nothing more. In the fire."

"Uh-huh. But what else? The pistol? Fingerprints? The camera? The roll of film? Tell me about the manor."

"Nothing at the manor. Anyhow, nothing of interest to us. We went through Martin's study. There were hundreds of prints, of course, but they were all Martin's or Ellen's—all of them. We examined the desk. All we found that just might have something to do with the case was a copy of a promissory note. Miss Lethander had loaned quite a bit of money to Martin against security of forest mortgages. There were a whole lot of letters and carbon copies in files in the drawer Mrs. Bernheim maintained the pistol was in. Nothing of interest, as far as I can make out."

"In the drawer where the pistol was?" said Durell, looking absently at Melander.

"Exactly."

There was a brief silence, then Durell spoke again. "Do you know if Martin Bernheim had a gun license?" he asked.

"Yes and no."

"What do you mean?"

"He had a license for a pistol, but he hadn't reported *this* pistol, and it wasn't in our register. On the other hand, he'd registered *another* pistol—the same type, a Beretta—but with another number."

"So you've checked?"

"Yes. If there's a license for the gun in Martin's room, then it's not with us. He acquired the gun illegally. At the moment, that's of little interest. But it's of much greater interest that there were clear fingerprints on it."

"That doesn't surprise me. I presume they were Martin Bernheim's. I mean, if it's murder and suicide, then the murderer doesn't go to the trouble of wiping off prints before he takes his own life, does he?"

"They're Martin's prints. But what do you mean, murder and suicide?"

Durell snorted. "That's what it was meant to look like. And to *that* extent the murderer had to cover himself. Cover up whatever he did to get Martin's prints on it. There really is a great deal that needs to be explained in this case. For instance, *the door was locked.* How the hell did the murderer get in? Or out? How did he gas Martin to death? How come he didn't gas himself to death at the same time?"

There was another silence, a long one, while Durell's fingers thrummed noisily on the desk. Melander sat still, watching him. Finally he cleared his throat and spoke.

"The camera, you said. The camera was empty. There was no film in the camera. Of the two rolls we confiscated, one was of Gittan in all her seductive glory and the other was unexposed. That was all. And only Victor's prints were on the camera."

"Empty, you said. Unexposed." Durell looked thoughtful. "If we look at it from a psychological point of view, when it comes to photographers, at least advanced photographers—and it looks as if Victor was one—wouldn't such a person put in a new roll of film as soon as he'd exposed the one already in there? Don't you think so? Isn't that likely?"

Melander nodded. "That's possible."

"Well," Durell went on, not without enthusiasm, "he actually *had* an unexposed roll, but didn't reload. What does that mean?"

His enthusiasm grew. "Listen to this," he added. "There was *another* roll of film in the picture somewhere. One that was in the camera, which the murderer took."

Durell's gaze hesitated on a blurred damp patch on the ceiling and then he said, "I wonder what can have been on *those* negatives?"

"But there were no prints on the camera," said Melander. "Except for Victor's."

"And there were no prints on the pistol," said Durell. "Except for Martin's. Sure you didn't expect our bright murderer to go around handing out calling cards?"

There was a knock on Melander's door, which was then opened discreetly by a police assistant, who looked in and said, "There's a call out here, concerning the Bernheim case —a lady on the line. Shall I put her through?"

Melander nodded and waited with his hand on the receiver. The phone rang. The chief of police pressed the receiver to his ear and Durell leaned forward to see if he could catch what was being said.

"Oh, yes," said Melander. "Yes, yes . . . we'll see to it . . . thanks for calling."

He put the receiver down, noting Durell's curiosity with amusement.

"That was the girl you thought was so bright upstairs—Vera Bernheim. She was reporting that her sister had an unpleasant experience late last night which may be connected with this other business. We ought to go out there—or, well, perhaps it's enough for one to go. What do you think?"

"What sort of experience?"

"That's what I think we ought to investigate."

"Then I'll investigate it," said Durell. "Can one of your boys drive me out there?"

He was already on his feet and Melander wondered which was the greater attraction, the experience or the girl who was so bright upstairs. But he hadn't actually finished his report yet. Not properly.

"You know, Bertil," he said, "despite everything, it's good to know this is in fact—well, I'd say almost *demonstrably*—a double murder. There's one thing I haven't had the opportunity to tell you yet, and it's probably crucial."

Durell had been heading for the door but now swung around and looked at his colleague.

Melander went on. "That pistol on the windowsill in Martin's room with Martin's fingerprints on the barrel—that pistol, you see, has nothing whatever to do with all this."

Durell's eyes widened as if he had been the victim of a practical joke. And yet simultaneously he began to understand, and the understanding filled him with satisfaction, because it finally removed *all* his doubts. He waited in silence for Melander to finish.

"The bullet taken out of Victor's heart," said Melander, "or, rather, out of his spine . . . was fired from a different gun."

Melander opened a drawer and took out a piece of paper, which he waved at Durell. The inspector went back to the desk, took the paper, and examined it closely, noting that it was a license and the registered gun was a Beretta—the same make as the pistol found in Martin's room—with a manufacturer's number ending in 3333. Without too much effort, he managed to remember that that combination of numbers was not the same as on the gun they had found. He handed the license back to Melander.

"As if that made matters any clearer—I mean, if the bullet was fired from *this* gun," he muttered to himself.

Twenty minutes later, he was shown into Miss Lethander's room. The old lady was there, but not alone this time. As if in her favorite place in the universe, she was once again over by the window, her back to the sky outside, more a silhouette than anything else. Vera and Veronica Bernheim were sitting in the yellow armchairs.

Durell was urged to take a seat on the sofa. On the table in front of him lay a flashlight with a long shaft—a powerful flashlight needing four batteries.

Veronica told her story, and then there was a long silence while Durell finished his notes in his black notebook, which by this point was beginning to overflow with facts, thoughts, sketches, and occasional doodles.

Another policeman was standing just inside the door. He had dumped a bag as black as Durell's notebook on the floor in front of him. Since Miss Lethander had not asked him to sit down, he was still standing there, to which he had no objection. If the old lady could stand, then so could he, and anyway it was just as well to keep his distance and take note of the impressions offered by his overall view.

Durell stopped writing and leaned back on the sofa.

"Now," he said, "why didn't you report this immediately? You must know—the night is long and it's very possible this person may have crept back up to the attic *again*, if he had to leave yesterday without completing his task. That was ill-advised of you. One should act *immediately*."

Vera was looking at him with amusement. He noticed this with favor as well as with disfavor. He liked her looking at him, but not that she was amused. That disturbed him. He liked people to respect what he represented. A policeman should enjoy the same respect as a doctor or a priest or a tax inspector. Vera did not look the least impressed.

"Aunt Lethander didn't wish to report the matter," she said.

"Oh, yes. Really?" Durell looked at the old lady in surprise. "Miss Lethander, did you think it was so unimportant? Considering everything else that has happened."

Miss Lethander did not reply at once. But when she did, it was in a firm, clear voice. "No, I didn't think it was unimportant. But I have to tell you that this event cannot alter anything that has occurred. My *family* is involved, Inspector. What happens in the family concerns no one else. We'll clear up all the horrible things that have happened here—but we'll do it *ourselves*. It has nothing to do with outsiders. Things have always been happening, good and bad, in this family, as in others. Allow *us* to deal with them. We want no interference."

Durell looked at her in surprise, hoping his mouth wasn't open, as it sounded like a declaration from the Middle Ages. For a few seconds his mind juggled the possibility that she was so shocked that she was trying to suppress what she didn't want to know, or that her arteries were so hardened she had no conception of what was at stake. But he abandoned both conclusions. She was not fuddled, either by age or by emotion. Instead, she might be the clearest-minded of them all, but possibly so experienced, or so sorely tried and disillusioned, that most of what happened around her became trivialities. He pointed at the flashlight.

"Miss Lethander," he said, "that is the flashlight you had in your hand when your . . ."

He hunted for the right word, but she found it for him before he was successful. ". . . when my great-niece came down from the attic. Yes. That was the flashlight. I heard her screaming and banging hysterically on the door. So I went out. The attic door was locked—well, the key was in the door, but it had been turned twice. Then I saw that flashlight on the floor just by the door . . ." As if she had guessed Durell's next question, she completed her statement. ". . . and it is not my flashlight, and I've never seen it before. It seems to me to be a very good flashlight."

Durell drew a deep breath. "Now we know that, then," he said. "All that remains is to go up and take a closer look at the attic." He turned to the policeman by the door. "Would you please take care of the flashlight?"

14

VERONICA

It was horrible having to go back up to the attic, and it made no difference that I was accompanied by two policemen and Vera, nor that it was the middle of the day and light was seeping in through the dusty skylights and dispersing the rather ghostly impression of murky passages and floating beams.

Durell asked me to reconstruct the course of events as best I could. I showed him how I had gone into the dressing room and how I'd pulled out the wooden box to tighten the bulb. Just as I was about to complete that part of the demonstration he stopped me.

"Stop!" he said. "Don't touch it. If it was unscrewed, there may be fingerprints on it. You said the bulb was warm."

"I know it was warm," I said. "It must have been turned on."

"Would you take care of the bulb?"

He turned to the second policeman, who hardly had to stretch to take out the light bulb. He put it on the floor, took a spray bottle out of his black bag, and then sprayed the bulb with powder. Then he looked at the result with satisfaction.

"There's some prints," he said.

"But I touched the bulb, too," I said.

He made no comment, but took out some Scotch tape and

fastened it to the bulb, and when he had done that, he put the bulb into a plastic bag and slipped it into his bag.

Later on, I was told that my prints *were* on it, but, blurred in the dust, they could see someone else had also held the bulb.

They asked me to go on. I showed them what I had done and how I had done it and where I had been. They were terribly interested in the place where the vanished shoes had been. The assistant with the bag crawled about on all fours, examining the floor with a magnifying glass. I could see he was looking for prints, but with no success, or else they were not clear enough, because he got up and took out a little battery-driven vacuum cleaner and cleaned up the whole area.

We went over to the tower room, the corner room. I showed them how I had put the clothes out on the bed and what I had done when the light had gone out. Durell walked around looking everywhere while I talked. He opened the door to the big cupboard and then closed it again. He looked in the washstand and told the other man to spray powder around the switch, then went over to the desk. Vera was watching his every movement with interest.

"Do you think he's hidden up here?" she said at last.

Durell gave her a swift glance. "He? What makes you think it was a he?"

She shrugged her shoulders, threw up her hands, and pouted.

"Of course I don't think anything," she said. "Do you think it was a she?"

He laughed and answered in the same vein. "Of course I don't think anything."

He bent down and examined the drawers and the top of the desk. His assistant sprayed them, too. With no result. Durell pulled out drawer after drawer and at the fourth, he stiffened suddenly, then let out a short, clear whistle.

"My, oh, my," he said, then, turning to the policeman, "Bring me a handkerchief."

He plunged his hand into the drawer and when he pulled it out again, he was holding a pistol at the very end of the barrel between his thumb and forefinger. He put it down carefully on the handkerchief the other man had spread out on top of the desk.

I shivered and tried to catch Vera's eye, but she was absorbed in the discovery. Durell gave instructions for the gun to be sprayed. The powder was like a white cloud around it. When one side had been done, he turned it over and gave it another shower. I heard him mumbling with satisfaction to himself. "Yes, indeed, there are prints . . . indeed . . . and . . . 3333 . . . this must be it . . . I think."

He stood up and turned toward us.

"Well, ladies," he said. "Not so dusty, this one. This gun belongs to Martin Bernheim, and if this isn't the murder weapon, then I'll eat my hat."

15

ELLEN

Miss Lethander and Alma went for their usual walk after lunch. Ellen saw them go, amazed that nothing seemed to be able to break this ritual, neither wind nor rain nor events that must be whirling through the old lady's mind. Ellen closed the window and decided to follow their example —maybe that was a way of escaping from it all.

She walked along the gravel road until she came to a felled area where logs had been stacked in neat piles and then left until the bark blackened and started to flake off. A grass-covered track wound its way into the forest, so she decided to follow that, and farther on, it turned into a path that became narrower and more overgrown until it disappeared alto-gether. She hesitated, thinking of turning back, but at the same time she felt a strong desire to continue straight into the forest, a ritual acceptance of silence and solitude. She fol-lowed her impulse and found she could walk between the hanging spruce branches and treacherous boulders hidden by the moss with far greater agility and ease than she had ex-pected. She came to a derelict half-rotten fence and walked along it until it suddenly ended in a dark stream, silently flowing along the edge of a bog full of bog myrtle, cran-berries, cloudberries, and sedge in tussocks of white moss. On the opposite side was the edge of another forest, rising up a steep fir-covered mountainside. But between where she was standing and the edge of the forest was a single tall pine, its roots exposed and curling like huge red snakes around immense boulders. She looked up the trunk and, at the top, in the almost dead crown, saw a bird's nest, an osprey's nest, and she remembered the previous summer seeing a pair of ospreys circling around the area, above the lake, diving down behind the treetops and swinging up again, gradually disappearing to some unknown place in the forest. It could have been here.

For a moment she thought she could hear the wing beats of that huge bird, the sound coming from behind her in an even, soft rhythm, but then she realized what it was. Footsteps. Softly running footsteps in the moss. She did not move, only turned her head and looked into the forest. Then she caught a glimpse of him between the trees and tangles of ferns, only about fifty yards away. He ran with light, elastic steps down to the stream, then stopped. She saw him raise his arm and with a violent overhand motion throw something small and black, which sailed out toward the lone pine tree among the boulders. For a few seconds he stood quite still, facing her, then he spun around and started running again, diagonally away from her, disappearing into the forest. She did not know whether he had seen her, but she had seen him and she knew who it was. Charles.

When she got back to the house and was going through the gate, she saw Ulla coming toward her with Lucy on a thin red cat leash. She looked awkward and uncertain when she stopped in front of Ellen, then she suddenly put her hand on Ellen's arm.

"Ellen," she said, "it's dreadful that I haven't said it before, but it's been an awful shock to us all. You must know how sorry we are for you, you poor thing."

Ellen forced a smile.

"Thank you, Ulla, dear," she said. "I haven't really taken it in myself yet."

"And all that awful business the evening before—but who could know?"

"No, who could know?"

Ellen felt almost sorry for her. She realized what it must have cost Ulla to make the gesture, but at the same time she suspected, slightly maliciously, it might be because Ulla was frightened. What was a complete catastrophe to her might well turn out to be just as threatening on Ulla's comfortable horizon.

Ulla bent down and picked up the cat. "There'll be a funeral, I suppose?"

"Of course there will. I haven't thought about it yet, Ulla —all the practical things."

"If you like, Fredrik and I will help you. We could ask Carl to drive us in to Gislaved and talk to an . . . an undertaker. When do you think it'll be?"

Ellen felt hollow inside suddenly. Why on earth should she start talking about this now? All those decisions to be made.

"I don't know," she said. "I'll pull myself together. Don't think about it anymore."

"Where are they now?"

Ellen forced herself to reply. "They've performed a postmortem, Ulla. It's a legal requirement whenever there's been a sudden death, whether relatives want it or not. They have to do to them exactly what you're doing to me now. Rooting around inside them to see what they can find. One doesn't own them anymore when things are like this, you see."

Ulla's eyes widened and she stepped backward, for without being aware of it, Ellen was apparently threatening her. Clearly Ulla was not alone in misunderstanding the gesture. The window in Mauritz's room opened and he leaned out.

"Steady now, Ellen," he said.

She turned to him in surprise. "It's nothing, Mauritz. Ulla was only trying to be kind to me."

"Only being kind," said Ulla. "I offered—said that Fredrik

and I would arrange the funeral. I'm sorry you feel that way about it, Ellen."

"Mauritz," said Ellen, following a sudden impulse. "Mauritz, dear, will you take care of it? Will you arrange everything?"

To get away from Ulla and the cat, she half ran over to him.

"Can I come in, and we can talk it over?" she asked.

He frowned, but closed the window and a moment later opened the outside door.

Mauritz's room was as much like her own as the two wings were like each other, but the color schemes were different. Here the carpets and materials were moss green, the furniture dark brown, and the wallpaper plain gray. In her room pale blue had been chosen, with unpainted pine furniture darkened with age to a golden brown, and pastel flowered wallpaper.

She sat down in one of the armchairs. It was good to sit down and she noticed she was tired after her walk in the forest. His presence gave her a sudden feeling of security. She was looked after in here and she felt the warmth inside her she had felt in the days when they had often met and relaxed —open and trusting.

"I wanted to get away from her," she said apologetically. "I'm sure you understand."

"Of course."

"There's so much to be arranged, but I can't think about it at the moment. I must get back to normal first."

He nodded. She gazed at him for a long time, searching for and finding the familiar little lines, expressions, and movements. He hasn't aged much when you really look at him, she thought. Small and slight, thin and sinewy, firm gray eyes which many people would say were cold, or at least cool. Under any circumstances they were intelligent, watchful and —at present she thought another adjective appropriate— suspicious. Although the air was warm and formal wear was

not expected, he was wearing a tailored shirt with long points
to the collar, properly buttoned at his slim throat, with an
elegant flowered tie that was in perfect taste.

"There's a lot to arrange," he said. "What are you going to
do with the manor? Keep it?"

"I don't know. I haven't thought that far. I can't keep the
horses, anyhow."

"Of course not. Can you go on living there?"

She bit her lip, unable to think of a reply.

"Ellen," he went on after a while, "would you be able to
look after old Aunt Lethander?"

"Look after her? I don't know what you mean."

"She can't stay here much longer. Alone. It wouldn't be
right to let Alma take all that responsibility in the long run.
It's an enormous house, for heaven's sake. She can't manage
forever."

"She's managed up to now. She gets help. She employs
people to help when necessary."

"I know. But that costs money. And it's not only that—it's
insane not to convert this house into something else."

"What do you mean?"

"Money."

Ellen felt extremely uncomfortable. Her hand shot out,
almost of its own accord, and she picked up the newspaper from the table. She started absently eyeing the head-
lines, trying to hide her discomfort. A row of numbers
was written along the top of the page, and in passing, almost unconsciously, she noted that the combination was
familiar.

"With all the contents and the actual site," he went on,
"it'd certainly go for about a million. The tax valuation is
over four hundred thousand and the fire-insurance valuation
double that. It'd be an excellent place for a foundation, perhaps, or a conference hotel. With some minor alterations, of
course. The problem is to get her to agree to it."

Ellen shook her head. "She'd never agree to it. She probably thinks we should wait. Do you mean she should move in with me?"

"Yes. Of course, you would be recompensed."

Ellen smiled slightly. "And you think the *others* would agree to that?"

"What do you mean?"

She stared at him, and then realized that he really did not understand.

"Do you think the Svenssons would dare abandon her to my care, with all the possible advantages to me that that might involve? And what about you, for that matter? Would you really take that risk yourself?"

He shrugged. "I'm used to taking risks. And I haven't suggested you should look after her affairs, because I don't think you're capable of that. Anyhow, no doubt you've got enough to do looking after your own affairs."

Ellen looked thoughtfully at him, a vague idea taking shape in her mind, but not yet sufficiently sharply for her to be able to grasp it. "Have you talked to Aunt Lethander about this?"

"No, not talked to her. But I've written to her to say I *want* to talk to her about it. And I had a try yesterday, despite all this uproar."

"Well?"

"No. She won't take up the matter. She won't even discuss it. She simply said no."

"Mm," said Ellen, smiling faintly again. "You'll have to count on her regarding you as a traitor from now on. That may have some consequences."

She sighed, put down the paper, and leaned back in the chair, almost serene. Then she suddenly sat bolt upright, snatched up the paper again, and held it out to him.

"Mauritz," she said, "why did you write our telephone number on the paper?"

He started, and for a brief moment a shadow flitted across his face. His eyes met hers and his look was so cold it frightened her. But her intuition was stronger than her fear.

"It was *you*, Mauritz," she cried. "It was you who spoke to Martin the day before yesterday. On Saturday—about four o'clock. It was you who phoned him."

They sat in silence for a long time, staring at each other, then finally Mauritz laughed and said softly, "Yes, I called Martin on Saturday. I wanted him to help me with this. Now Martin's gone and I thought I'd ask you instead."

"What did Martin say?"

"He said he thought we ought to discuss the matter. He said he had an interest in doing so himself. But on one condition."

"What condition?"

Ellen felt weak, wanting to get up but not having the energy to do so.

"He wanted fifteen thousand."

She had known that was what he was going to say before he said it.

"Did he say why?"

"Up to a point, yes. He said it was a matter of blackmail. Victor needed the money. Immediately."

"Did he say what the blackmail was about?"

There was silence before Mauritz spoke again.

"He told me what it was about," he said. "It was a letter."

He suddenly flung out his arms. "Unfortunately, then it was too late for us to meet and discuss it all. Poor Ellen. And poor Martin and poor Victor."

"You know that that letter—it was from Stella?"

"I realized that," he said. "Stella wrote a lot of letters—a lot of silly and unnecessary letters. And then she died. You know, don't you, Ellen, that Stella killed herself?"

He got up suddenly and started walking up and down the room. Then he stopped at the window and stood there, immobile, looking out, as if gazing into space. Ellen suddenly felt sorry for him. How lonely he was, really. Perhaps as lonely as herself at this moment.

"Since then . . ." she said tentatively, "has there been any woman in your life, Mauritz?"

"My daughter. Only my daughter. Malin is really the only woman I've ever loved—friend, comforter, group therapist, problem solver, secretary, my daughter. Stella was the great lie and hell in my life."

He turned to her and smiled coldly.

"You find that out afterward, you see," he said. "Perhaps you'll do the same about Martin."

Ellen nodded. "Maybe so. Perhaps you're right. Anyhow, I won't go looking for anyone else. Perhaps one should—should have, at least."

She remembered something and went on. "You knew a girl—goodness knows how many years ago—when you lived here. Do you remember? I remember you were very much in love with her. Wasn't her name Britt? I remember her parents—heavens, it's ages ago. You should have chosen her instead of Stella."

She stopped and looked up at him, for she had noticed that what she was saying had had a very peculiar effect on him. She saw that he was suddenly extremely annoyed, a dark flush creeping up from his neck and across his face and forehead. She got up.

"May I take the paper with me?" she said. "It'd be nice to relax with the crossword."

"Please do."

She put it under her arm. "Do you know what happened to her, to Britt Hansson?"

"No, no idea."

Ellen knew he was lying, and she was overcome with a mixture of amazement, discomfort, curiosity, and suspicion, because she could not understand why he would.

When she got outside, fortunately Ulla had gone. But a police car was just coming through the gates, so she hurried over to her room.

16

CHARLES

When the intercom in Melander's office clicked, both the tall policeman standing in the middle of the floor and his red-haired Stockholm colleague seated in one of the armchairs sensed the tension rising.

"We've got him here now," said the voice on the intercom.

"Good. Bring him in."

Melander walked over to his desk and switched on the tape recorder, turning the microphone to face the room, then started to dictate: "Interrogation of Charles Sixten Svensson, detained on suspicion of murder of Martin and Victor Bernheim, Monday, etc., etc. . . . please fill in date and time." He glanced at his watch. "The time is three twenty-five P.M. Officiating at interrogation . . . fill in my name there . . . and Inspector Bertil Durell. No other witnesses present. Interrogation recorded on Tandberg tape recorder . . ."

At that moment the door opened and a policeman showed Charles into the room and gave Melander a swift, questioning look, which he answered with a signal that they were to be left alone. Charles remained standing just inside the doorway, looking around uneasily, his chest under his open shirt rising and falling faster than it should in a well-trained athlete. He had on a pair of tight, flare jeans, and his broad brass belt buckle winked in the sunlight every time he moved.

"Please come over here, Charles Sixten Svensson," said Melander. "If you'll sit here, that'll be fine. We have switched on the tape recorder, and naturally you must think carefully before answering any of the questions I am going to ask you. Do you understand?"

Charles looked frightened and confused, but nodded and at once went over to the desk and sat down. Melander went around and sat down opposite him.

"Now, let's get this straight. You've been told that we suspect you may have something to do with the murder of Victor Bernheim and Martin Bernheim. The police assistant told you that, didn't he?"

Charles nodded.

"They said I was a suspect," he said in a low voice. "They said I was under arrest."

Melander smiled at him.

"No," he said. "You are not under arrest, but you have been detained for questioning, and if you can give us satisfactory answers to our questions, we'll let you go. You must understand that. Do you?"

Charles looked dejectedly down at the desktop in front of him.

"What do you want to know?" he said. "I haven't got much to tell."

"Just tell us what you know, a lot or a little. Would you first tell us in your own words what you were doing on Saturday evening. When you were having a party in the house."

"You know that already," he said. "I know Gittan told you everything."

Melander looked patiently at him. "Your own words, Charles."

"Okay, I know what you want. You want to know that I knew what they were up to."

"Who? Up to what?"

"Up in the attic . . ."

He paused and seemed to be trying to remember, then he glanced timidly around and went on at Durell's encouraging nod. "We were having this party, then—eating and drinking a little. I didn't drink much, since I don't want to get out of shape, but the others were drinking quite a bit. Then I noticed Gittan had disappeared somewhere with Victor. They'd been messing around all day and I was damned annoyed about the whole thing. I snooped around for a while to see if I could find them—then I got a tip from Malin. She asked me why I was snooping around like that and said if I was looking for Gittan, I should try up in the attic."

"And you did?"

He nodded, his hair flopping over his forehead. He pushed it back and went on quietly. "Yes, I crept up there. I could already hear them on the stairs, laughing and so on. There were no lights on, except in the corner room, and the door was open, so I could see exactly what was happening."

"What was happening?"

"You know what was happening."

He sounded suddenly sharp and hostile, as if he thought there was no need to torment him by going through all this stuff they already knew all over again. But then he decided to tell them.

"Victor was taking photographs. She was stripped. When he'd taken a lot, he pulled her down on the bed and . . . undressed . . . took off his trousers, I mean. I didn't see any more because I was so angry everything went black."

"Why didn't you go in and raise hell?" said Durell. "Didn't you dare?"

"No, I didn't dare," said Charles, turning his head and glaring at Durell. "I didn't dare because I don't know what I would've done. But don't think I was scared of tackling him. There's been a lot of talk about him throwing a punch at me, and that if I'd gone on, I might have been beaten up then, too. But that wasn't what I was afraid of. I went downstairs instead. I thought it was . . . thought I'd think it over. Break up with her or something—or talk to her—or, well, do something, anyhow."

"You haven't been married long?"

"Six months. A hell of a mistake."

"What kind of mistake?"

Charles looked at Melander and actually laughed, a hard, sneering laugh. "That chick's as different from what I'd thought she'd be as could be. But she's . . . well, you've seen for yourselves. She's damn good looking, and much too damn good in bed and . . . well, I'm hooked on her—totally."

"Still?"

He nodded silently.

Melander went on. "Well, what did you do then?"

"I went down to our room—the room on the first floor. The party was over. I knocked on Carl's door and asked him to come in. I wanted to talk to someone about this."

"So you told him."

"Not everything. Only about the photographing. I couldn't get the other part out, because I thought it was so damned—well, sordid." He paused, then added harshly, "but no doubt Carl damned well realized."

"Uh-huh. And then?"

"Well, then she came down, too. Carl left, and she wanted to go to bed."

"And you. You went to bed, too, of course."

"No. I changed and went out. I needed to run some of it off, I thought."

Durell had not said much, but now he rose suddenly and went over to the desk. He stood beside Charles and said mildly, "In that weather? There was a thunderstorm, wasn't there?"

"No, not then. It had stopped raining. Well, there were a hell of a lot of puddles on the road, but what the hell. When I want to go out running, I usually don't bother about the weather. If I did, I might as well stop altogether."

"But it was dark."

"So what? You can see when your eyes get used to it. But that's true—it was dark."

There was a long pause. Melander picked up a pen and

fingered it thoughtfully. Durell stood still, looking not unsympathetically at the young man in the uncomfortable chair in front of the tape recorder. Charles's eyes were focused on some vague spot on the desk.

"And then?" said Durell.

"I came back, of course—but wait a minute." He looked up as if suddenly remembering something. "Yes, a car passed me as I was on my way back. If you don't believe me, you can find the driver. He must've seen me. He could testify."

"Passed you?" said Durell sharply. "Are you sure you didn't *meet* a car?"

"Certain."

"Where was this, roughly?"

"Five, maybe six hundred yards from the house. It must've . . ." He appeared to have been struck by the thought for the first time. "It must've been on its way up to the house, right?" He looked first at Durell, then at Melander. "That road doesn't go anywhere else."

Durell nodded. "That's right. Now, then—this car. Were its lights on?"

"Yes, of course."

"Did you see what make it was?"

"No, no idea. I wonder who the hell it could've been, anyway? Maybe it was Victor. Maybe Victor was trying to get hold of me. But then he would've stopped."

"Why would he be trying to get hold of you?"

"I don't know. Perhaps Gittan . . ."

"Perhaps Gittan what?"

Charles looked nervous and dejected.

"I mean, perhaps Gittan had told Victor I'd gone off and he . . . that she'd said something about . . . about being scared I'd do something stupid . . . jumping in the lake or something like that . . . hell, you know how women are."

"Yes, indeed."

Durell accepted the opinion and simultaneously rejected both it and the preliminary theory.

"Now, then," he said. "Now you're home again. What did you do then?"

"Went to bed. Undressed and got into bed."

"And Gittan?"

"She was asleep. I think so, anyhow."

There was a silence, Melander's eyes fixed on Charles's face, Durell still standing by the chair, swaying back and forth slightly.

"Do you know why we've brought you here?" he said finally.

"You said I was under suspicion. You wanted to question me. I suppose this is what happens when someone's a suspect. It's just as well you know all this now."

"Not all. No, Charles, you haven't told us everything. There's one more matter we'd like you to explain. We've found the murder weapon, you see. The gun Victor Bernheim was shot with."

"Oh, yes . . ."

Charles looked up and met Durell's eyes.

"We found it in the attic. In a drawer in the desk there. And do you know what, Charles? Do you know what else we found? Your fingerprints—not the slightest doubt about it—on the barrel. And now we'd like you to account for how they came to be there."

Charles looked like an animal suddenly finding itself in a trap. For a long while he sat immobile, apparently not breathing, his eyes rigidly focused on some indefinite spot in the room. Then he said in a thick voice, "You're bluffing."

"No, Charles, we're not bluffing."

There was silence again, Durell and Melander waiting patiently as they watched the silent struggle going on inside young Svensson. He was very pale, his mouth moving faintly, apparently trying to shape words, but not daring to let them out.

"If you don't speak soon," said Durell finally, "then I'm afraid we will have to draw our own conclusions. You were very upset that evening. No doubt you had reason to be. Do you want to know what we think happened?"

Charles sat up and drew a deep breath, staring straight at Durell's expressionless face. The inspector felt like a snake paralyzing its prey by its very presence.

"I think," he said slowly, "I think you went out running, just as you said, and I also think you went back to your room and maybe even to bed. Then I don't believe you any longer. No, Charles, when you lay there thinking in the dark, your whole being filled with jealousy and misery, listening to your wife's untroubled breathing beside you in the bed, you suddenly couldn't stand it any longer. You decided to get revenge. Or, rather, you decided to settle the matter. One way or another."

Durell paused as he tried to see what impression his words were making.

"So you crept out of bed again," he went on. "Perhaps you even got dressed. Then you went upstairs to the third floor and knocked on Victor's door. Victor had not yet gone to bed, although it was late. I'd say it was about two o'clock in the morning. Well, Charles, Victor opened the door. I'm not sure he would have if he'd known you were outside. Perhaps he thought it was someone else—why not your wife, for instance? And Victor, being what he was, couldn't resist the temptation to find out whether it really was her. Or miss the chance of a renewed little adventure *if* it was her. So he opened the door. You pushed your way in. It's possible Victor didn't have much respect for you—I mean, he wasn't afraid of a fight if necessary. He even knew karate, I've been told. On the other hand, it's dangerous playing around with people who are wildly jealous, because you never know what they'll do— knives and all that—so he made no immediate attempt to throw you out. Instead he went back into his room, sat down in an armchair, and, as a little warning, took out a pistol he had in some way or other got from his father. Then he offered to listen to what you had to say. I have no idea what or how much you said, but we do know what you did. You managed to get hold of the pistol and you shot Victor. It's possible a court might bring in a manslaughter verdict, since you certainly didn't have the pistol with you when you went up there. You know, the opportunity makes the thief. But in that case you must be a little more cooperative when it comes to clarifying the course of events."

Durell took a box of throat lozenges out of his jacket pocket and put a lozenge in his mouth as he thoughtfully regarded Charles sitting there, still silent and immobile.

"Well, what happened next?" said Durell. "I imagine you were very upset when you realized what you'd done. You put the pistol in your pocket. You turned off the light, took the key, left the room, and locked the door from outside. You were just going to go back down to your own room when you suddenly came face to face with Martin. The shot had woken him up. You managed to find a plausible explanation, and finally you and Martin went into his room together. In an unobtrusive moment you slipped Victor's key into Martin's dressing-gown pocket. You talked for a while before leaving the room, and when you eventually did, you'd managed to do one more thing. The fire had died down. You pushed the damper in. Then you left and Martin locked the door behind you. Although you couldn't be absolutely certain, there was a good chance that that witness would be silenced pretty quickly. And it worked. Martin will never testify against you."

Durell fell silent and looked pityingly at Charles, then added, "Admit that that's what happened."

Charles shook his head, his hair flopping again.

"You tell me instead why I didn't shoot Martin, too," he said. "Wouldn't that have been much more natural?"

Durell frowned heavily and tried to look thoughtful. Then he snapped his fingers.

"Ah, yes," he said. "I forgot to say that *before* you ran into Martin, you'd had time to slip up to the attic and hide the gun. That was it, Charles. You no longer had the pistol on you. So what choice did you have? Gas was not a bad alternative."

There was another pause, but Durell noticed, and so did Melander, Charles's attitude beginning to soften, and suddenly he started talking as if someone else were handing him the words and all he had to do was speak them.

"I'll tell you," he said. "I didn't do all that. But I—yes, I was up there. But it was all different. You see, I'd decided when I was out running. I had to get hold of those photographs he'd taken of Gittan. I couldn't stand the thought of him having them, and maybe selling them, and her being a centerfold in one of those damned rags. I thought about it all while I was running—then I decided to go up and make sure I got that roll of film. That's what I did."

"Uh-huh," said Durell, nodding. "And he didn't want to hand it over, and then what I've said just happened, is that it?"

"No," said Charles. "First, I went up as soon as I got back. It couldn't have been later than twelve-thirty. And, second, he let me in just like that. He didn't even seem surprised."

"So . . ."

"He was—he was almost friendly. Not at all like when other people are around—you know—scornful and provocative and swinish. He asked me to come in. When he opened the door, he said, 'Oh, Christ, it's you, is it—what do you want?' 'Give me that roll of film,' I said. 'What film?' he said. 'The photos you took of Gittan,' I said. 'They're not going anywhere,' I said. 'No, of course not,' he said. 'Come on in and we'll talk about it.' So he let me in and went and sat down in the armchair, while I stood on the other side of the table, between the table and the door, that is. 'Sit down,' he said. 'Christ, no,' I said. 'All I want is the film.' That self-confident attitude of his—he wasn't even *annoyed*—well, it made me uncertain, almost, I don't know . . . but . . . anyhow, the gun was on the table and I didn't even know if it was loaded. Anyhow, I picked it up and aimed it at him and said, 'For Christ's sake, Victor, give me that film before I pull the trigger—you've got five seconds.' He got up, went and grabbed the camera, took the film out, and handed it to me. He was even laughing as he gave it to me. 'Here you are,' he said. 'If it means that much to you, you can damned well have it. Please put that gun down, since it could easily go off with you as shaky as you are right now.' Well, I took the film and put the pistol down and left the room. That's what happened. I never fired it. I would never have fired it, even if he'd refused to give me the film."

Charles fell abruptly silent. There was no doubt that he was very relieved.

"And where is that film now?" said Durell.

"I've destroyed it."

"How?"

"Thrown it away." His face brightened. "I've even got a witness to that. Ellen Bernheim. If you don't believe me, ask her. I threw it away today, when I was out running."

"Would you be able to find it again? Or show us where you threw it?"

"Roughly. I don't know exactly where it landed. It might have gone down a bog hole."

"Uh-huh."

Durell paused, letting his pale blue eyes rest on Charles.

"Have you told this to anyone else?" he said suddenly. "Carl, for instance?"

"No."

"And that car, the one that passed you—do you know what time it was then?"

"Sometime after midnight—maybe nearer twelve-thirty. I'm not sure."

Durell let this sink in while he thought, then he whirled around, crossed the room, and sank down into the armchair he had been sitting in when Melander had been in charge of the questioning.

"Good, Charles," he said. "You can go now."

Melander looked at him in surprise, but without protesting he pressed the intercom button and asked for someone to come and show Charles out. When the young man had left the room, not entirely without relieved astonishment, Melander leaned over the tape recorder, looked at his watch, and said, "End of interrogation. The time is now four o'clock."

Then he turned off the machine, leaned back in his chair, and looked at Durell.

"Do you believe all that?" he said.

"Every word of it. Charles may well be involved in some other way—but he didn't murder Victor. No, he certainly didn't."

"Pity," said Melander, chuckling. "I thought it sounded very convincing, your description of what happened. But there you are, and that film business seems correct. There was no film in the camera and according to your reasoning, there should've been if Victor was a professional."

Durell waved his hand dismissively.

"Not just that," he said. "There was nothing to stop him from first shooting Victor and then taking the film—Victor could easily have refused to hand it over. No, it was the fingerprints."

"Charles's? On the gun?" Melander raised his eyebrows.

"Exactly. *If* he had fired the gun, he could have acted in two ways—either flung the gun away willy-nilly and gone off in a panic of some kind—*then* one might have expected those lovely prints on the barrel. Or else it could be that he took the gun with him to hide the evidence—or make it more difficult for us to go any further. Without the murder weapon it's difficult to get anywhere in court. Well, if he'd done that, and hidden it in the attic, then it's absurd that he didn't first wipe off the prints. Or even make an effort to wipe them off. And furthermore, if Victor refused to hand over the film and Charles shot him, then took the film out of the camera himself, why weren't there any prints on the camera when there were some on the gun? And why didn't he take the pistol into the forest and throw it away when that was how he disposed of the film? No, my friend, the only logical version is the one Charles himself has just given us."

"But—someone else might've taken the gun and hidden it in the attic before he had an opportunity to wipe off the prints. I mean, perhaps he kept the gun somewhere, wondering what to do with it? Oh, forget it." Melander sounded apologetic.

"There's more to come," said Durell patiently. "If he came out of the room and ran into Martin, and Martin had heard the shot, do you think Charles would've had the chance to go into Martin's room and sit down in peace and quiet to discuss the matter?"

"No, he wouldn't."

Durell put his head to one side, then went on. "Well, don't say that. Martin might have been relieved that someone had murdered Victor. You know, Martin had a motive for getting Victor out of the way. Just *why* Martin took that gun with him that evening"—Durell paused—"we don't really know."

"What the hell are you getting at?" said Melander. "Are you joking?"

Durell looked at him pensively. "Not at all. But don't you think Charles would have fired again if he'd been pressed? He wouldn't have had time to hide the gun in the attic before Martin came out to see what was going on. So all that business of closing the damper and poisoning Martin was really rather farfetched, wasn't it? At least, if he hadn't planned it all beforehand."

"But supposing he *had?*"

"You mean that he already had the gun with him when he went upstairs? You mean he'd stolen it earlier? From whom? From Martin? Or from Victor? Victor *actually knew* Martin had the gun and it's possible he got it from Martin—or had stolen it sometime during the evening. No, my friend."

Durell shook his head doubtfully. "Charles didn't have a gun with him when he went up to Victor. That seems incongruous. So let's accept that it really was in Victor's room when Charles got there. But then—"

"Yes, yes," interrupted Melander, and there was no mistaking the irritation in his voice. "Then he should have shot Martin, too, and not closed the damper."

"Exactly." Durell paused. "You know, we mustn't forget this poisoning business probably had only one purpose behind it, and that was to make it look as if Martin had shot Victor and then gone back to his room to take his own life by closing the damper. That's where the prints come in."

"What prints?" Melander looked bewildered.

"Martin's, of course."

Durell sucked on the throat lozenge. "You were the first to know that the gun we found in Martin's room had excellent and easily identified prints from Martin's right hand. So that was supposed to be the murder weapon. I suppose it was a bit naive to think we'd believe it, but on the other hand there was the off chance of there not being too much technical investigating if everything looked neat and tidy and logical. Do you follow me?"

Melander nodded uncertainly. "So you mean the fingerprints . . ."

"Exactly. This is one of those rare cases when fingerprints exempt the suspect instead of convicting him."

He smiled with satisfaction, but Melander still seemed somewhat bewildered. "You mean Martin's fingerprints . . ."

"No, no. I mean Charles's, of course. And I mean that the murderer presumably knew—the murderer almost certainly knew—that Charles's fingerprints were on that gun. Do you follow me?"

"But . . . but . . ." Melander was even more confused. "You said it was made to look as if Martin had murdered Victor. Murder, then suicide. Martin's prints were on *that* gun . . ."

"Yes, yes," said Durell impatiently. "On *that* gun, yes.

That was a mistake on the murderer's part. When the murderer discovered his mistake, it was, of course, an unpleasant surprise. On the other hand, he had the right weapon under control. And not only that—it was equipped with a very suitable calling card."

At last he had finished the throat lozenge, and he went on more or less to himself. "If that's so, then we have a reasonable explanation for someone snooping around in the attic and frightening his fellow creatures out of their wits. Someone. Someone who knows his way around so well that he even knows the whereabouts of the fuse box."

Then he sighed. "But any of them could have known that. They're all like children of the house, all of them."

He got up out of the armchair. "I wonder if they've gone yet. I think I'll go back to the house with Charles."

17

ULLA

ULLA'S WORLD COLLAPSED WHEN CHARLES WAS TAKEN AWAY. As the car drove through the gate she stood on the steps in a blur, leaning on Fredrik's arm and trying to persuade herself the just-visible dark silhouette in the back window was someone else.

Gittan was also upset.

"They can't force people to go with them like that," she said. "It's horrible of them just to take him away and leave me alone, and anyhow he hadn't the slightest idea Victor and I . . ." Her words went on pouring into Ulla's ears, but Ulla was unable to comprehend them, for her own emotions were blocking any kind of sensible thought. Ulla squeezed Fredrik's arm.

"Shouldn't we get hold of a lawyer?" she said. "They think —don't you see?—they think Charles did it."

For once, Fredrik had nothing against her suggestion, which made her unhappier than ever. But when the car had gone, he suddenly put his arm around her shoulders and led her back into the house.

"Lie down for a while, Ulla," he said. "Take a pill and lie down on the bed. I think I'll go to the kitchen and . . . I'll have a drink, I think."

So he left her alone, clearly unaware that she didn't have a single pill left. She lay still on the bed, trying to disperse her thoughts, but her anxiety kept washing through her, and in the end she could stand it no longer. She got up and sat on the bed. Then she remembered Aunt Lethander would almost certainly have something. She glanced at her watch, for however much her nerves were tormenting her, or her emotions warring inside her, she was still aware it was Aunt Lethander's nap time, and she was sure that not even what had happened these last few days, however disturbing it had all been, would change that routine. It was almost four o'clock. Maybe she could risk disturbing her now.

She got up, and as she left the room it struck her that this was almost an exact replica of Saturday's excursion, when Fredrik was supposed to have spoken to Aunt Lethander but had ended up instead in Martin's room, from which she had seen him emerge seething with rage. As she crept through the hall she felt slightly faint with dismay, and she hurried on until she found herself standing in front of the closed door to Aunt Lethander's room. She put her ear to the door and listened. Yes, Aunt Lethander was awake. She could hear her talking in there. She was not alone, either, and Ulla was curious. She pressed her ear even closer and heard another voice. It was Alma's. Disappointed, she stood up again and knocked on the door, but instead of the expected summons there was silence inside. A few seconds went by. Then the key turned in the lock and Aunt Lethander was standing in front of her. Her voice was harsh as she spoke.

"What do you want, Ulla? You know it's my nap time."

Ulla did not know what to say, stammering in some confusion that she'd heard Aunt Lethander was awake, and she had to have a tranquilizer of some kind and Charles had been taken away by the police. She was very relieved to notice that Aunt Lethander understood and retreated into her apartment, to return again a minute or so later with a wonderful little red pill, which she said would calm her down and allow her to sleep. Ulla knew that was true because she had used the same kind before. Then Aunt Lethander closed the door again. Ulla heard her turning the key, locking the door. Without bothering to get any water, she put the pill in her mouth and swallowed it, then crept back to her room. As she closed the door she saw Fredrik coming along the corridor with a glass in his hand. She stopped, thinking he was on his way in to her, but he wasn't. She heard his steps approach, pass the door, and finally fade away as he crossed the soft carpet in the hall. She lay down on the bed with a deep sigh of satisfaction, waiting for the peace that would soon spread through her nervous system.

18

VERONICA

CHARLES RETURNED AS UNEXPECTEDLY AS HE HAD LEFT. VERA and I had been playing badminton on the lawn, and Ellen was sitting reading in an uncomfortable garden chair. While we were playing she read aloud what the newspaper had to say about the Double Drama in the haunted country mansion. Although many of the details were familiar, none of it seemed to have anything to do with us or the events. Vera just laughed.

"Mansion!" she said. "The things they say."

While I was wondering whether the old house could be called a mansion or not, she took the opportunity of winning the point by smashing the shuttlecock to my feet. Ellen put the newspaper on the table.

"Do you remember that conversation on Saturday when Martin said you had phoned me?"

Vera lowered her racket, but before she could reply, Ellen said, "You said you knew you hadn't called, and you hadn't, either. It was Mauritz."

"So what?" said Vera, waiting before serving.

"Do you think I ought to tell the police?"

Vera did not look at all interested and got ready to serve. "I think you should tell the police everything you think is of interest. And I have a feeling you think this is."

At that very moment a police car drove up to the front of the house again, and Charles stepped out of the back, followed by the inspector. Ellen got up. Durell at once spotted her and waved more familiarly at us than was appropriate, I thought, and when we waved back, he quickly came over to us and actually shook Ellen's hand. But I had the impression it was not so much Ellen or his duties he was concerned with, but Vera, for while he was still holding Ellen's hand his eyes were on her.

He can't be falling in love with her, can he? I thought. The poor creature. At the same time, I noticed Vera looking steadily at him from behind her huge glasses, definitely not uninterested, and also slightly amused. Ellen didn't notice. For her, his arrival was an answer to her uncertainty. She drew him across to the garden chairs and asked him to sit down. Then she told him about the telephone call. He looked at her with approval.

"I'm glad you told me," he said. "I'd thought of having a talk with Mauritz Corn, and this gives me a good excuse. Did you find out what he wanted from your husband?"

Ellen nodded and told him, but as I was rather far away, I didn't catch all the details, although I realized it was about Aunt Lethander and the blackmail story, that fifteen thousand. Then Ellen revealed how she had discovered it was Mauritz who had phoned. She went in to get the newspaper, showing him the telephone number jotted down at the top. I was curious and went closer.

"I noticed he really didn't like it when I asked about Britt Hansson," she said. "I had a feeling he was lying."

"Really," said Durell, looking at her blankly. "Then I must ask him why. Do you have any idea?"

"No," said Ellen. "It was only intuition, and you must take that for what it's worth."

"Intuition," said Durell. "Intuition is a kind of insight, too, although the connection can't always be clearly seen. A great deal of the truth comes to light, Mrs. Bernheim, when you start scraping away at what you first thought was intuition—or *only* intuition, as you put it."

He leaned back in his chair and read the newspaper with care. I thought he was looking very satisfied as he calmly and methodically folded the paper and put it in his jacket pocket. Then he got up and turned to Ellen.

"Do you by any chance know where she is now, this Britt Hansson?" he said.

"I have no idea," said Ellen. "But her parents still live here. His name is Birger Hansson and he's a farmer. They live a few miles away from the manor."

"Good," said Durell. "Then I'll take a chance. Let's go in and make a telephone call, Mrs. Bernheim. Her parents are sure to know where I can get hold of her, and it's better to do one thing too many than one too few. Don't you think so?"

Vera and I watched them walk away and then appear again in front of the house, Durell walking briskly and purposefully up the steps, Ellen following more hesitantly. But perhaps that was just my impression. Perhaps she was only more indecisive, more unsure about what it was he really wanted to know.

19

MAURITZ

Mauritz Corn did not look surprised when he opened the door and asked Durell to come in. He gestured toward an armchair and invited the inspector to sit down. Durell did so and waited until the other man sat down opposite him, on the other side of the table. He noted, not without envy, that Mr. Corn's tie was definitely one up on his own, with its large rose-colored flowers and thin lines of emerald green against a black background. Mauritz appeared calm and relaxed. Durell took that to be a sign of personal self-confidence or, alternatively, the practiced attitude of an experienced businessman—for he must have been *somewhat* curious.

"Mr. Corn," Durell said quietly, "you drove down from Stockholm last Saturday night, didn't you, and arrived here in the morning, just after it was discovered that something was wrong in the two Bernheim gentlemen's rooms? Isn't that so?"

Mauritz nodded.

"Then, if I've got it right, you contacted Martin Bernheim sometime on Saturday afternoon. You spoke on the telephone."

Mauritz nodded. "That's so. I suppose Ellen told you." He smiled slightly maliciously.

"That's correct," said Durell. "Now, then—where were you

calling from? Was it from your office in Stockholm or from your home?"

"From my office. I had a number of things to arrange before I could come down here."

"I see. This telephone call—so it was to make certain arrangements for an old people's home or some such for Miss Lethander, and you wanted Martin Bernheim's cooperation?"

Mauritz nodded. "Generally speaking, that's right, yes. Martin was not unwilling, but he wanted—how shall I put it?—he wanted to borrow a sum of money before he would help. Fifteen thousand kronor. He explained that he personally did not want it, but Victor did."

"You say he *wanted* to borrow money. Wasn't it a *demand?*"

Mauritz shrugged his shoulders. "All right, then, let's say he demanded it."

"And what was your reaction to this demand?"

"I thought we could at least discuss it. I offered to. When I got here."

"Which would be Sunday?"

"Exactly."

There was a short silence, during which Durell noted that the other man's expression showed nothing. He went on. "So you weren't expected until Sunday?"

"No."

"Wasn't Miss Lethander expecting you? I understood there was an empty chair left for you all through the luncheon that was the start of this drama. Wasn't it slightly pathetic to make such an arrangement if you weren't going to meet until Sunday?"

"Maybe so. I'd told her I might be delayed. The delay was longer than I'd predicted."

"So at first you had originally intended to come on Saturday? You never told her it might not be until the following day?"

"The idea was that I'd come sometime over the weekend, and that is what I did. I know Aunt Lethander was expecting me on Saturday. But that was Aunt Lethander's opinion. I think she just thought up that empty-chair affair on purpose. Old ladies can be absurd."

"Maybe so."

Durell paused again and took the newspaper out of his jacket pocket.

"This newspaper," he said. "You wrote Martin Bernheim's telephone number on it. Did you get the number from the telephone directory?"

Mauritz looked uncertainly at him, apparently not really understanding the question. "I got the number from the operator. I don't like to look up numbers in the directory. The print's so small I always make mistakes."

"So you wrote the number down in your office?"

"Yes, that's right. I don't really see what you're getting at."

"Well . . ." Durell put his head to one side and screwed up his eyes a little. "I think it's a little peculiar that you brought the newspaper with you. It's Saturday morning's paper—and you left late in the evening. That's a bit odd, isn't it?"

Mauritz made a gesture with his hands and propped his elbows on his thighs. "I usually do the crossword puzzle, you see, Inspector. Saturday's paper has one of the best puzzles in the country. At least, I think so. Things have kept getting in the way, so I haven't done this one, but if you wouldn't mind leaving the paper here, I'd be grateful. Perhaps I'll get a chance to do it now."

Durell spoke almost apologetically. "I'm very sorry, Mr. Corn, but you're lying to me. You didn't bring this newspaper with you from Stockholm, and you didn't call Martin Bernheim from your office. In itself, it's not really important which you did, but I don't understand why you're lying."

Mauritz stiffened, and Durell saw he was making a sudden effort to keep control, and that he was succeeding, too. His voice was still calm when he spoke. "I really don't understand what the hell you mean when you say I'm lying."

"Listen to me, Mr. Corn. On this newspaper is a number, and of course that number changes every day, since it's the code number of the day. And after that number—you can see for yourself . . ." He leaned across the table with the paper held out, pointing at the number just below the paper's title. "Here are three small stars. You see, that means this paper was sold—not in Stockholm but somewhere else. In Jönköping, for instance. And since you must have bought the paper before you wrote Martin Bernheim's telephone number on it, you can hardly have called him from your office but must have called from, shall we say, Jönköping, for instance. And now I want to ask you—*why* do you maintain you were in Stockholm when Martin Bernheim was murdered when, in fact, you were somewhere else?"

He suddenly straightened up and said sharply, "Perhaps even here *in this house?*"

Mauritz Corn was silent. Durell realized he was desperately trying to find something to say, but Durell's expression also told him that lies would be unlikely to combat the shower of questions he would now be exposed to. So as not to lead him into the temptation to continue lying, Durell went on in an almost friendly tone.

"If you were in Jönköping when you telephoned," he said, "and I happen to know that you were, since you have a lady friend there who in fact told me—and if you actually stayed with her quite late that evening—may I then ask, why didn't you come over here? Why didn't you at least take part in the evening party since you had missed the luncheon?"

Mauritz laughed dryly and ironically. "You've already said why. I have a lady friend in Jönköping. I thought it more pleasant to spend the evening with her. So you've spoken to her, have you?"

"Yes, I've spoken to her. I telephoned her and had my suspicions confirmed. She also told me you left her as early as about eleven."

He let the words sink in.

"Where did you go afterward?"

Corn sat in silence for a long time, gazing into the air as if trying to find a way out. Then he spoke.

"It was hellishly stupid of me," he said slowly, "not to have told you the truth in the first place. Sooner or later it was bound to come out. I'll tell you the whole truth, Inspector. Since I don't have anything to hide about Britt anymore, there's nothing else to hide. No, I have nothing to hide."

He sat in silence again before starting to talk, and when he did, he spoke swiftly and surely, perhaps deliberately quickly to increase his credibility.

"I drove down from Stockholm on Saturday afternoon to celebrate Aunt Lethander's ninetieth birthday, yes, but as you know I had other things to do, and I had in fact already warned Aunt Lethander in a letter beforehand. I was thinking of spending the night with Britt and then coming here on Sunday. It struck me on the way down that it might be a good thing if Martin helped me with my plans for moving Aunt Lethander and selling the house, so I decided to telephone him when I got to Jönköping. It was true we hadn't spoken to each other for many years, but this was business, and—well, I phoned him."

Durell broke in like lightning. "How did he react?"

"React? He was slightly surprised, of course. But when I outlined it briefly to him and he heard what it was about, he—well, he thought we might as well discuss the matter. He said he was going to spend the night at Aunt Lethander's because there was bound to be liquor around and he could hardly drive back the same night. He always had a room in the house at his disposal, anyhow. So we decided to get together on Sunday morning. Then I drove back to Britt's."

Durell interrupted him again. "Where were you calling from?"

"From a tobacconist's." He smiled slightly. "From the same place I bought the newspaper. Shall I go on?"

Durell nodded.

"So I drove back to Britt's and had dinner there. I had agreed with Martin that I'd call during the evening to confirm that he was interested. It turned out to be . . . a matter of . . ."

Mauritz became uncertain, so Durell spoke. "It was a matter of?"

"Martin said he would discuss the matter, on one condition. That fifteen thousand—he wanted it then and there, in cash."

"As a loan? Or once and for all? Regardless of how the operation worked out?" Durell had managed a surprised expression, hoping Mauritz would notice.

"A loan against a receipt was roughly what I'd thought. Unfortunately, I couldn't raise that amount in such a short time, since no banks were open, and I didn't have enough in my account."

"So you had to talk to Britt and ask her to make up the rest? Was that what you meant?" asked Durell, without expression.

"Yes. Of course I had to ask her first. If she would or could."

"And did you get the money? Or a check?"

"No. But, of course, I suppose you know that already."

Durell smiled. "No, I didn't, actually. But it's not hard to check that sort of thing, so I believe you. So—you were expecting this conversation with Martin?"

"Yes, but he never telephoned. At about eleven I telephoned him but couldn't get through. There was something wrong with the telephone—or, rather, the line was cut off—you know that."

"Yes, yes. I know. May I make a guess, in fact, the guess that made me come here to talk to you slightly more confidentially, Mr. Corn, even before I knew about your trips here and there and your evasions. You drove here that night. You got here at about half-past twelve. And you occupied this room without anyone having the slightest idea you were here. Isn't that so?"

Corn nodded, "Yes."

Since he was also looking bewildered, Durell expounded. "You were seen, you see. You passed someone taking some exercise at that time of night."

He paused.

"And then," he went on in a low voice, "you contacted Martin Bernheim?"

Mauritz Corn paused before answering for a tenth of a second too long for Durell not to realize what had happened, and when Mauritz saw this, he extended the pause even longer. Then he spoke again.

"Yes," he said wearily, "I met Martin. I parked the car outside the stone wall. As I was on my way here I saw Martin on the steps of the house. He was alone. I went up to him and shook his hand. He smelled of liquor but wasn't drunk. I asked him why he hadn't called me, and then he told me he had tried but hadn't been able to get through. 'But we can talk now,' he said. We went into my room."

"And then? You talked?"

"Yes."

"And the money? What did he say about your not having brought the money?"

"He said it'd be all right if I could guarantee to get it by Monday—today, in fact. I promised to."

"And this other business—did you come to an agreement? Were you going to move the old lady?"

Corn nodded. "He promised to help, yes. He offered to have her at the manor, provided he was compensated." Corn smiled. "Poor Martin, he'd do anything for money. I don't think there's much left of that estate."

"And then?" said Durell. "What happened next?"

"He stayed about half an hour. Then he left. It's funny, but in some way it was as if we had never really been apart. I mean, it didn't seem like years since we'd last met."

He smiled sorrowfully. Durell got up slowly and drew a deep breath, apparently fully understanding the other man's nostalgic melancholy.

Then he said as honestly as he was able to, "You've been very candid and cooperative with me, Mr. Corn. I've only got a few more questions to ask you today, if you don't mind?"

He gazed in a troubled way at the floor, trying to look modest. "The first one is . . . The first one is whether Martin said anything about the contents of that letter which Victor knew the value of so well. Do you know?"

Corn shook his head slowly. "As far as I can make out, it had something to do with Stella—she was my wife."

Durell nodded sorrowfully. "I know. Martin had had some kind of affair with her."

"Yes. I imagine he didn't want Ellen to know about it."

"So she knew nothing?"

"She may have known. But the letter may have contained— how can I express it?—painful details. All that should've been forgotten by now."

"That's right. And the other question, Mr. Corn, is about the fifteen thousand kronor. That's a lot of money. Was Martin's assistance with moving Miss Lethander really so important that you were prepared to pay fifteen thousand kronor for it?"

Corn swallowed slowly. "There was the commission money on the sale of the house—I'd thought of undertaking the sale myself. And . . ."

"And?"

"And it could also have been regarded as a kind of payment to Martin for taking on the responsibility of her—of the old lady, I mean. And . . ."

"Yes. And . . . ?"

"And I've had a guilty conscience for a hell of a time about Martin. I had a front man buy an oak wood off him. For next to nothing. I made a bundle from it. If I could help him with fifteen thousand, then that'd make me feel better."

"Did he know you'd cheated him?"

"It slipped out by mistake when I telephoned him. I thought he'd known for years."

"And now you're telling me because you think Martin may have told Ellen, for instance, so I would already know about that oak-wood matter?"

"No. You must see that I only wish to be honest."

Durell looked very thoughtful.

"My last question, Mr. Corn," he said. "Did you sense that what was to happen between you and Martin that night might be a question of life and death?"

Mauritz Corn had suddenly turned very pale, his cheek muscles twitching beneath his skin.

"Nonsense!" he said. "What the hell are you getting at, anyway?"

"It's just . . ." Durell went on patiently. "It's just that after Martin had had that telephone conversation with you—when you called from Jönköping, I mean—he put a gun in his pocket. He may have done that in order to kill you or to—well—to stop you from killing him."

Durell smiled slightly, making an effort not to reveal that he had noticed at once the other man's reaction, and, pleased with his confrontation with probably the last person to see Martin alive, he left the room.

20

VERA

"So you saw Charles throw something away?"

Ellen nodded.

"Not only that," she said. "I also saw almost exactly where it landed. There's a kind of little island of large boulders in the marsh, and there's a tall pine there. It fell in among the rocks, below the pine."

"Would you be able to show me the place?"

"My dear Inspector, I don't know if I've got the energy to walk all that way again today. But—wait a minute, Inspector."

She got up out of the garden chair, making a sign to Durell to follow her, and together they walked across the gravel, now a copperish hue from the afternoon sun. She stopped by the open window and called to Vera, who was evidently in the bathroom. Durell stayed discreetly in the background while mother and daughter talked and he heard Vera laugh. Then she vanished from the window and Ellen came back.

"Vera will go with you," she said. "She knows exactly where that pine tree is. She'll be with you in a few minutes."

While he was waiting he went across and sat on the front steps, but had hardly sat down when he heard the front door open and someone come down the steps behind him.

"You're wanted on the telephone, Inspector."

He recognized Alma's voice and got to his feet.

"The telephone's in the hall," she said. He followed her into the house and picked up the receiver. It was Melander, and he sounded excited.

"Bertil, we've had a visit from a very interesting witness. His name is Adolf Werner, and he was on duty at the Bernheims' stables the night Martin and Victor were murdered. Do you know what he said?"

"Maybe," said Durell. "Did he say he saw a car drive up to the manor sometime between one and two o'clock that night?"

There was an astonished silence at the other end.

"How the hell did you know that? Have you been talking to him, too?"

"No, but I've been thinking. Did he say anything else?"

"Yes. He was curious about who it might be, so he went up to the house and looked around. There was a light on in Martin's study, he said. He crept up and looked in to see if some uninvited guest was taking the opportunity to help himself. And he *saw* the person in question clearly. Do you know who it was, Bertil?"

"Let me guess." Durell paused for effect, imagining Melander's impatience at the other end of the line. "Was it—was it Martin?"

"But—how the *hell* could you know that? You must have talked to Werner."

Durell laughed. "No, but I've been thinking . . . The time fits, doesn't it?"

"He wasn't sure what time it was. He was asleep when the car woke him up. He didn't look at his watch."

"It doesn't matter," Durell said. "Did he by any chance see if Martin had anyone with him?"

"No, he was alone. At least he didn't see anyone else there."

"But what about in the car? Someone might have been waiting in the car."

"I asked him that, too. He didn't look in the car. When

he saw it was Martin, he saw no reason to investigate further. So Werner went back to the stables and back to bed again."

"Did he see what Martin was doing?"

"No, he was by his desk."

"You see?" said Durell, then, changing the subject suddenly, he asked, "Have you heard anything from the handwriting expert?"

"Not yet, but we're expecting to any time now."

"Call me when you do, will you? I've got my ideas about that, too. You know, I've been thinking . . ."

He laughed at the sound of Melander's groan. Then he replaced the receiver and went back outside, where Vera was already waiting for him.

Durell felt a shiver go through him. Her legs were bare and she was wearing a dark brown leather skirt and a plaid shirt with the sleeves rolled up. He noted she had applied a little makeup, just enough for his taste. She came to meet him, and even took his arm as if to demonstrate that he was indeed to come with her, and in that way they walked out through the gateway and along the narrow gravel road, where she suddenly dropped his arm.

"How far have you gotten with all this?" she said, immediately regretting the question and smiling apologetically at him. "If you're allowed to say anything," she added, "without disobeying regulations."

"You're not a suspect," said Durell dryly. "Neither you nor your sister could possibly have had anything to do with this matter. But otherwise we haven't gotten particularly far."

He said nothing for a long time, listening to the gravel crunching beneath their feet.

"Sometimes I think I've caught a glimpse of the truth," he went on. "Then some irrefutable fact or other arises and that's enough for us to have to start all over again and try to find new angles of approach. Ah, yes. A great many coincidences have combined to make this dish especially well spiced. A great many sophisticated details in the method of approach. A great many motives. A great many people. A great many statements. A great many lies. And actually only an occasional opening. But those that exist are difficult. And yet . . ."

He stopped, sighed, then took up the thread again.

"You're not unintelligent, Miss Bernheim," he said. "Let's go through the facts together. That might help me sort out our thoughts. Now, then, we know a little about the actual timetable. Victor was shot at about twenty past two, according to the two Bokströms, who heard the shot. There is nothing to contradict that statement, as both the autopsy and medical report accept it within a margin of about an hour on either side. As far as your father is concerned, the margin is the same, and we're fairly sure he died after Victor, in any case. About an hour or so afterward, perhaps. We also know that Charles went to see Victor at about twelve-thirty and that Mauritz and Martin met up in Mauritz's room at about one o'clock. We also know that after that meeting, Martin felt called upon to drive home to the manor, where he was observed by a trustworthy witness sometime between one and two. That nighttime visit is also a reason for us to ask a vital question: What was so important that he made that trip in the middle of the night? What so clearly absorbed him that he even left his keys behind? Do you have any idea, Miss Bernheim?"

She shook her head. "No," she said quietly. "But I'd appreciate it if we could use first names, provided it's not against regulations. Could it be that he wanted to check if what Victor had said was true, that he, Victor, I mean, really did have that letter—let's call it the Stella letter—or whether he was bluffing? For instance, Victor might well have known it existed, perhaps had seen it and read it at some point, without actually having taken it?"

"Why, then, didn't Martin check when he was at home earlier that day? He already knew what it was all about, didn't he? And that was when Ellen saw him looking in his desk drawers and when he took the gun. No, I think you're wrong there, Miss—er, Vera. It must have been something else. And very likely something else that was actually there in the desk drawer, since he forgot his keys on the desk. I wonder what."

"Perhaps there was a copy?"

Durell considered the possibility and decided it was perhaps not unlikely. If an original letter was worth fifteen thousand, then a copy would not be totally uninteresting. He was just about to approve the suggestion when Vera went on.

"I think there's another important question," she said. "Aside from the reason why he drove home in the middle of the night."

"You think so?" said Durell, sneaking a surreptitious look at her and finding her ear a very agreeable shape.

"Was he alone? Could anyone else have been with him in the car?"

"No one was seen, anyhow. And who would bother to investigate the car? When our witness saw a light on in the window and wanted to find out if anything was wrong, and then saw that it was a perfectly legitimate visitor—that is, Martin himself—he just went back to the stables."

She smiled. "The witness? You mean one of the Werner boys? But then you don't actually *know* whether he had anyone with him?"

"Who might have been in the car then?"

"Anyone." She shrugged her shoulders. "How would I know?"

"No, how would you know?"

Durell pursed his lips. "But to go back to the timetable. Mrs. Bokström—Charlotte, I mean—witnessed Martin's departure, and she also saw him come back. That was at about two. So we can call that time the last bell—time for the curtain to go up on this drama. Twenty minutes later, there was a shot. And an hour or so later, Martin was also dead. Have you any idea what the play was like?"

Vera glanced swiftly at him as she turned off the road down the grassy track into the forest.

"Someone knocked on Victor's door," she said. "Victor let the person in, which he should never have done."

"That's absolutely right. So we have to ask ourselves—why did he let that person in in the middle of the night? And also—why was he still up? Charles had left the room at least two hours earlier—anyhow, an hour and a half earlier. And if we start from the fact that he gave us a truthful account of his activities, which I am inclined to believe, then the most natural thing for Victor to do was go to bed . . ." Durell stopped and explained. "You should perhaps know that we got a lot from Charles today. That's what I'm referring to. Now, then —Victor sits up for quite a long time, in the middle of the night, not even putting a new roll of film in his camera, although he seems to have all the time in the world. He didn't read a newspaper or a book, for none was found there. Nor did he write anything or think up anything else to do, as far as we can make out. He just sat there, meditating."

"Victor was not the sort to meditate."

"No. Waiting, then. What was he waiting for?"

Vera made a face. "Perhaps he'd agreed to meet someone? Anyone—one of the girls, maybe?"

"Not bad," said Durell, nodding approvingly. "Victor liked girls. But he couldn't have been wanting a woman all that badly, since he had satisfied his desires only a few hours earlier."

Vera looked at him with interest but no surprise.

"You don't know Victor," she said. "Maybe Gittan came back. Maybe they'd agreed on that?"

"Hardly."

"You mean she was much too well guarded by Charles?"

"Not just that. We have to think of someone capable of murder—of shooting someone. I don't think that girl is."

Vera smiled. "Yes, you're right. In her case it would be a question of teeth and claws. Well, what about Malin? Victor wasn't indifferent to her, either. And she wasn't entirely un-interested in Victor. And I can't imagine *that* girl being afraid of using a gun."

Durell shook his head again. "First of all, she's recently married, isn't she? She doesn't seem to be the kind of person to kick over the traces on a lighthearted impulse. Second, she wasn't with Victor when the shot was heard. We know that. Charlotte Bokström saw her in her room—saw both her and her husband through the window—only seconds after the shot. Charlotte thought they had gotten up to find out what it was all about, like herself. No, give me a better suggestion."

"Perhaps it wasn't a girl at all. What about Fredrik?"

"Fredrik? That's possible. Though what reason would Victor have for letting Fredrik in his room in the middle of the night?"

"A nightcap, perhaps?"

"No liquor in the room."

"No, of course, you've thought all this through. But—are you sure it wasn't Martin?"

"It wasn't Martin. Or Ellen. Or Veronica. Or you. That I'm sure of."

"How sure?"

"As far as Martin's concerned—perfectly sure. Because Victor wasn't shot with the gun we found in Martin's room with Martin's fingerprints on the barrel, and because Martin was also murdered and didn't commit suicide, which it was meant to look like, and the key to Victor's room had been put in Martin's dressing-gown pocket for the same reason, and the real murder weapon was found up in the attic with different fingerprints on it, and the damper was open although it should have been closed and . . ."

"The damper was open?" Vera stopped and clutched Durell's arm.

He nodded, seeking her eyes behind the glasses. "Yes, in-deed. Martin died of carbon-monoxide poisoning, and yet the damper was open. Martin was supposed to have taken his own life with the aid of a glowing fire, and yet the damper was open."

He fell silent. They walked on, the path narrowing, the moss getting thicker at every step.

"So there are only two alternatives," said Vera. "If the damper ever *was* closed, someone must have opened it. Either Martin himself or someone else. But since the room was locked from inside, another person can be excluded. So *Martin* must have realized he was being poisoned by carbon monoxide, noticed the damper was closed, opened it, and yet still succumbed to the gas. The other alternative is that the carbon monoxide came into the room *even though* the damper was open."

She stopped, then said eagerly, "Could anyone have tampered with the flue from above—from the roof?"

Durell looked gravely at her.

"No," he said. "Unfortunately, my dear Vera." He flushed slightly when he heard himself inserting the totally irrelevant endearment. "No one has been on the roof. And no one could possibly have managed that, in fact. But you're right when you say there is the alternative that carbon monoxide got into the room although the damper was open—such things have happened before. You can, for instance . . ." He stopped, as it seemed almost treacherous to reveal techniques and methods many of his colleagues would consider professional secrets. But he felt the need to complete the sentence, and as he did, it gave him a feeling of almost indecent intimacy. "For instance, fumes from a car engine."

Vera nodded. "I was going to suggest something like that. But that doesn't really make sense, since I can't imagine it'd be possible to carry that out with so many people in the house—I mean, anyone taking such a risk—how would it work? It's utterly unbelievable."

"Yes."

He sighed heavily. He would have given a lot to be able to

produce an explanation, a brilliant, dazzling explanation that in one stroke would make everything fall into place with astounding clarity, not simply to satisfy his professional ambitions but also to impress her, a realization that made him feel weak in the knees.

They walked on in silence for a while, the first bluish tinge of approaching dusk spreading through the trees, contours of the ferns growing softer and clearer, as well as on the boulders lying everywhere, their gray surfaces thickly covered with moss. Then they came to the stream and out of the marsh rose the tall pine and the abandoned osprey nest at the top. Vera took off her shoes.

"To be on the safe side," she said, smiling. "I don't know how used you are to stepping on the right tufts, but if I were you, I wouldn't risk it in those shoes."

She laughed. Durell hesitated for a moment, then resolutely sat down on a fallen tree and undid the laces of his oxblood-colored shoes. He took them off and placed them on the tree trunk, then took off his socks and rolled up his trousers.

"Let's go," he said delightedly. "No doubt it'll tickle the soles of my feet, but a discarded roll of film is worth it."

Five minutes later, they had found the film, lying exactly where Ellen had said it was, just below the pine tree, between a couple of boulders. He slipped it into his pocket and they went back to the stream.

"There is one thing it might be useful to discuss," he said suddenly. "The motive. Have *you* given it any thought?"

Vera looked at him absently as he pulled on his socks, a slow process, since his feet were wet.

"Motive?" she said. "First of all, could there have been *one* motive for Victor and *another* for Martin? When Victor was out of the way, perhaps it became . . . I mean, if Martin caught the murderer at it, that would be sufficient motive."

"Exactly," said Durell. "That's what I thought. The rooms are next door to each other. Martin simply must have heard that shot. Anything else is unthinkable. Also, everything points to the fact that he was awake, even though it was so late. Perhaps *that* isn't all that peculiar, since he'd been back to the manor. Now, then—this is what I thought. Say the murderer had just shot Victor. He leaves the room and runs into Martin. Martin asks what the hell's going on. The murderer tells him to calm down and suggests they go into Martin's room to talk about it. Somehow he manages to explain the shot and Martin accepts the explanation. But the murderer realizes he has gained only one thing—time. The murder will soon be discovered. He seeks a way out of the situation which is really the only one. Martin must be wiped out."

He paused. "And so Martin was wiped out."

Vera looked skeptical.

"Brilliant," she said. "But *how* did he succeed in calming Martin down? What *kind* of explanation did Martin accept? *How* could he stop Martin from going into Victor's room to investigate what had happened? I know Martin, I'll have you know. Martin never let anything go unexplained. Martin always followed up everything, for good or bad. No, that isn't what happened."

She suddenly looked so pensive that Durell almost regretted trying anything so crudely provocative.

"But it *would* be possible," she said. *"Either* that Martin *knew* Victor was going to be murdered—that he was simply an accessory, even though he himself was eliminated later ..."

Durell was filled with warm tenderness, and to him Vera's cropped, noncommittal hairstyle seemed to have become illuminated from within and transformed into a shining halo.

"And the motive?" he said.

"The letter, of course—blackmail—*or ... or ...*"

"... or," prompted Durell breathlessly.

"... or that Martin wasn't in his room, so he never heard the shot at all?"

He couldn't resist any longer. He got up from the fallen

tree with one shoe on, the other in his hand, and he went over and embraced her.

"Vera," he said. "You . . . you . . . my name's Bertil. I forgot to tell you. Vera, I've never met anyone who . . ."

She was standing rigid in his awkward embrace and he thought her immobility was like a pendulum standing still, impossible to say which way it would swing, and he became aware of the fact that he was standing there with a shoe in one hand, pressed against her back, and one stocking-clad foot becoming more and more soaked from the moss of the muddy edge of the stream. But he didn't retreat. Suddenly it happened. Slowly she withdrew from him. Then she raised both hands and placed them behind his head and kissed him, softly, intently, absorbed. What she said filled him with the most marvelous expectations.

"Bertil," she said, "do you think . . . could it possibly have been *Aunt Lethander?*"

21

DURELL

Dusk was just beginning to descend as he left her at the door. She held out her hand to him, which he took to be secret confirmation that they would meet again, not only to discuss a murder case but for something that was in his view much less routine. Perhaps they would go to the opera together. Perhaps he would have the opportunity to excavate from deep down in his bureau some of his buried romances—the texts, melodies, and songs of Bertil Durell—horribly difficult to sing, with long sequences in the top tenor ranges. He tried to remember a suitable exponent, found the melody, but at first not the words. When they suddenly came back to him, he rejected the piece in question: "an impression you left on my heart/when I placed it tenderly in your hand/its pulse a trembling dart/its warmth a glowing brand."

He flushed slightly and, straightening out his jazzy tie, said, "Thank you, Vera, for that inspiring run-through of the case. I really think you've given me several ideas to follow up."

She laughed and opened the door at the same time, but before she got any further, Veronica appeared behind her and saw Durell. She was wearing a cardigan and was obviously on her way out.

"The police are looking for you, Inspector," she said. "They asked you to contact Mr. Melander as soon as you can."

He nodded. "Is there a telephone in your room?"

"No," said Vera. "You'll have to use the one in the hall."

She pointed toward the house, nodded good-bye, and vanished into the room as Veronica passed him. She turned off onto the lawn, where, two hours earlier, he had interrupted their game of badminton.

Durell went into the hall, dialed the number, and asked to speak to Melander, who was not slow to pass on the news.

"We finally got a report from the handwriting expert," he said. "On those burned fragments of the letter. They were in real ink, not ball point. Do you know whose handwriting it is? Almost certainly?"

"I think so," said Durell. "Miss Lethander's."

There was silence on the other end for several seconds.

"Still playing hide-and-seek, I see," said Melander at last. "Okay, you're right. As far as we can tell, the old lady wrote the letter."

Durell was satisfied, but did not want Melander to think his bull's-eye had been sheer chance.

"You see," he said, "who writes in ink these days, except old and conservative people?"

"Yes, you're right, of course. Well, I thought—"

Durell interrupted him. "Who'd guess you'd fall for that?"

"Fall for what?"

"That 'old and conservative' business. Who says the *letter's* not old? In the old days there *was* only ink."

Melander groaned. "I thought, since you're already out there, you might as well have a talk with her at once."

"Good idea. I'll talk to her right away. But—the idea that it might be her—I got that about half an hour ago in the forest. So I would've talked to her anyhow."

"In the forest?"

"Forget it."

He put down the receiver. As he thought over how he was going to put the questions, he slowly climbed the stairs to the second floor, his hand sliding along the banister rail, the surface as smooth as velvet, worn by thousands of hands along the centuries. When he got to the top, he met Alma coming along the corridor from Miss Lethander's room. She seemed to be in a hurry, but when she saw him, she stopped at once and said good evening to him. Then, with unnecessary agitation, or so it seemed to Durell, she said, "How long are those rooms going to stay sealed up like this?"

"Until further notice," said Durell. "Don't you like it? Does it remind you too much . . . ?"

"No, it's not that," she said. "It's just that I'm longing to clean up in there, because until that's done the house won't be as it's always been."

Durell looked at her with curiosity. She was dressed in her spotless housekeeper's outfit, which made her look a lot like a nurse. He had a sudden thought.

"Tell me, Miss Gren," he said. "You lit the fire in Martin Bernheim's room last Saturday, didn't you?"

"Yes."

"When was that?"

"While the party was on. It must have been between ten and ten-thirty, I'd say."

"Was it a big fire? I mean, there was quite a lot of ash."

"Just ordinary, and all the old ash had been taken away when I laid it. But maybe I should tell you that I filled the copper scuttle, too. There was plenty of wood if Mr. Bernheim had wanted to put on any more."

"I see." Durell nodded. "Another question—what about the damper? Was it fully open?"

"Of course." Alma sounded offended and her voice was harsh as she said, "If the damper hadn't been fully open, the fire would've smoked dreadfully. I know that from experience. Especially on a day like that, when it was raining and there was a thunderstorm. No, Inspector, you can be sure the damper was properly open."

"So sometimes that fire smokes in bad weather?" said Durell. "Is that right?"

"If the damper isn't fully open, yes. But it was."

"Do you think . . ." Durell hesitated before asking the question, but then decided to go ahead. "Do you think it is possible for carbon monoxide to collect in the chimney and then seep back into the room in that kind of weather, if the fire isn't burning all that high? I mean—you must have considerable experience with fires, I presume?"

"Yes, I have." She nodded, slightly flattered by the admission and now considerably more friendly.

"Wasn't the damper fully open," she said, "when you found Mr. Bernheim in there? That's what I've been told."

"Yes, it was fully open."

"Then it's not possible for the smoke to have come down again." Her answer was resolute and definite. "That's a very good open fire. In all my fifty years in this house I've never once heard of it smoking. And it didn't even smell from the balloons when I lit the fire, and that was right at the start, when it's at its most sensitive. I mean—before the heat is drawing in the chimney. And rubber can smell so nasty."

"The balloons?"

Durell looked blank, although he knew perfectly well what it was all about.

"Yes, there were some popped balloons up here in the hall —the young people had left them about. I picked them up and put them on the fire, once I got it going."

She suddenly looked at the clock on the wall and exclaimed, "Oh, my goodness, I really must go and make dinner now, if there's nothing else I can do for you. Look, it'll soon be seven o'clock."

"Dinner will be late," said Durell, smiling.

"We always eat late in this house. Miss Lethander often traveled to France when she was younger, I'll have you know."

She started walking toward the stairs, then suddenly stopped, turned around, and looked suspiciously at him. "By the way, what are you doing up here, Inspector?"

"I was just going to have a few words with Miss Lethander, if that's all right."

He could have sworn she looked worried.

"I don't think Miss Lethander will see you at the moment," she said. "I've just come from her room. She didn't even bother to answer when I knocked. But, of course, you can always try."

She turned around again and waddled down the stairs, ponderous, large, but still with a certain litheness of movement.

Durell went on through the dining room to Miss Lethander's apartment. Somewhere in the back of his mind he noted that the door to the stairs leading from the corridor down to the kitchen was open and he wondered vaguely why Alma hadn't gone that way if she were in such a hurry to start preparing dinner. Then he found himself outside Miss Lethander's room and he knocked cautiously once, then again, and finally considerably harder. But she did not answer. Then he tried the door handle, but the door was locked. He sighed. Even an ancient lady needs to be alone and undisturbed sometimes, he thought. Perhaps she was sitting in her negligee at the dressing table, putting on her evening makeup. So he would just have to be patient. Perhaps he could wait in one of the sealed rooms to which he had access, sit in an armchair in peace and quiet, and try to lure from his surroundings a few answers to some obscure questions.

But he did not go into a sealed room. Instead he sat down in the large armchair by the window, and as he sat there thinking, an undefinable unease began to descend on him, prickling his skin and warning him of what he was vaguely aware was going to happen. He should anticipate it. Forestall it. Prevent it. But when he had come that far in his thoughts, the mists closed in on him again. He took out a throat lozenge and pensively put it in his mouth.

22

VERONICA

I COULDN'T HELP WONDERING WHAT VERA AND THAT LITTLE redheaded policeman had been up to in the forest. I knew Vera so well, I could see at once she was interested in him, and as far as he was concerned, he must have felt like a confused schoolboy as he stood there holding her hand just that much too long for him to discover that it was just that much too long. I laughed to myself, hoping they wouldn't notice as I went out, especially hoping they wouldn't realize why. That could easily have been painful, and as far as I was concerned, I wished them well in whatever it was I might wish them well in.

I started collecting the badminton rackets and shuttle-cocks, and putting them back in the box, because I had been well drilled by Ellen that if there was anything Miss Lethander really disapproved of, it was things being left around at night. So I started taking down the net, which was when I heard the cat. I could hear Lucy miaowing loudly and persistently behind the house, as if she'd mistaken the season. At first I didn't take much notice, but when she went on, I began to suspect she'd gotten stuck somewhere. I remembered what it was like when Ellen's cats—she had had several when I was young—had climbed up a tree or had been chased up by a dog and then had not dared climb down. That was what Lucy sounded like. I dropped the net and went around to the side of the house. The cat was now miaowing louder than ever. I could hear definitely now that it came from the ravine behind the house. I ran across to the wire fence that had been erected along the edge of the cliff to stop people from falling down there in the dark. The wire mesh was so fine I was surprised the cat had been able to get through it.

I stared down at the boulders and rocks at the bottom. It was getting dark now, but not so dark that I couldn't distinguish the boulders and clumps of bracken and juniper bushes growing down there. Suddenly I saw the cat. She was sitting on a large rock, yowling heartrendingly up toward the house. At the same time, I heard something else. The wind had risen, and I could hear a window diagonally above me banging backward and forward. I couldn't see it from where I was, since the fence stopped me from going any farther, but a little farther on, the fence curved away and I could get a better view of the façade of the house from there. So I walked along it and then saw it was Aunt Lethander's window swinging loose. I was suddenly filled with foreboding. There was something insistent and nagging about that banging noise, and, mixed with the wailing of the cat, it grew more and more menacing and ominous.

Then I saw something alongside the rock the cat was on, something dark and ill defined, almost like a blue-black shadow. Slowly it became a human body, a woman's body in a long dress, a woman with white hair and a deathly pale, still face. I realized immediately that it was Aunt Lethander, that Aunt Lethander was lying down there among the boulders, and Lucy's wails grew louder and louder until they pierced my head like an unbearable siren, the banging from the window thundering in my ears in the same rhythm as the beating of my own heart. I don't know how long I stood there, becoming increasingly aware of what I could see and hear, but although at the time it seemed to be several minutes, I still think I reacted much more swiftly. I started to scream. At the same time, I could feel the tears rising and blinding me.

Then suddenly Carl was beside me, and Malin, and the Yugoslav, then Mauritz and Vera and Ellen. Carl leaped over the wire fence, so softly and skillfully that, despite my state of mind, I noticed it with some surprise. Then the Yugoslav jumped over, and both of them started clambering down the mountainside. A moment later, they were beside her and lifting her up. She looked as light as a feather. Then I noticed with surprise that I wasn't watching them but looking around for the cat, wondering what it was going to do, but then I realized Lucy had disappeared. When they got up to the fence, they handed the lifeless body over to Charles.

"She's dead," said Carl.

Charles carried her over to the lawn and carefully put her down on a blanket someone had spread out on the ground, and then Ellen was there, taking Aunt Lethander's pulse, and Malin was gently straightening out her clothes just as the red-haired policeman came rushing toward us. When he arrived, he bent down and stared at her intently for a few seconds. Then he turned the silvery head carefully, as if trying to find traces of something, an injury of some kind. He let the head sink back against the blanket and placed her arms down at her sides with the palms upward. Then he felt her fingers, bending and straightening them lightly, and ran his own hands lightly down the sides of her body. He stopped at the left pocket of her dress and took out a key, which he held up and examined closely in the failing light. It was beginning to grow dark up there, too, now. Then he put the key in his jacket pocket and got up. He asked Malin to phone for an ambulance, then suddenly said, "Who found her?"

I replied that I had.

"Would you point out the place to me, please?" he said.

He went with me to the fence. While I told him about Lucy miaowing and how I'd thought something had happened, and how I'd looked down and suddenly seen her down there, then started screaming—while I was telling him all this he also became aware of the window up there, still swinging backward and forward. He did just what I had—went along the fence until it curved away so that he could see the side of the house. I went with him. He made some notes in his black book, despite the increasing darkness.

"Let's go wait for the ambulance now," he said quickly. He told Charles to pick Aunt Lethander up again, as carefully as he could, and take her into the house. As Charles climbed the steps to the front entrance with the old lady in his arms, and all of us, silent and shocked, trailed behind him, Alma suddenly appeared in the doorway. I saw in some confusion that she had Lucy in her arms, and in the light from the lamp above the door, the cat's eyes were glowing, like phosphorescent globes.

23

DURELL

DURELL TOOK THE STAIRS IN A FEW BOUNDS, MOVING MUCH more nimbly and swiftly than would have been thought possible. He went without delay straight to Miss Lethander's apartment and tried the door handle. He found the door still locked, just as it had been half an hour earlier. He looked at his watch. In fact, it was not even that long. Only a quarter of an hour. He listened against the door, trying to hear whether or not the banging of the window could be heard through the door or the wall, because on his previous visit he had heard nothing. Now he could hear it, but only faintly. The illogical conclusion raced through his head that Miss Lethander might have fallen down the precipice *after* his previous visit, but he at once dismissed it, for he was not *certain* that it had been sufficiently windy then to make the window swing.

His trained eye and experienced hands had also told him—and the medical officer's examination would confirm it—that Miss Lethander had probably been dead a couple of hours before her body was found. The color of her face indicated that, as did the early signs of rigor mortis in her fingers and elbows. But that wasn't evidence that the actual *fall* hadn't occurred later, of course. And since a dead body doesn't fall of its own accord—if *that* was correct—then someone must have helped. Durell smiled grimly. Why would anyone have helped when Miss Lethander *was* already dead? To make it look as if she had fallen? To explain certain injuries—blows on the head, for instance? But if she *hadn't* been dead when she fell, then it must have happened a couple of hours ago, and so the window had also been open during that time *without* banging, which must mean it *hadn't* been particularly windy only a quarter of an hour or so earlier.

He sighed with dissatisfaction, but allowed it all to come full circle. He took out the key he had found in Miss Lethander's pocket. It was the right key. He established that the door was locked with a double lock, requiring two turns. He opened the door, felt for the light switch, switched on the light, and went into old Miss Lethander's apartment.

Everything was exactly as he remembered it from his previous visit. He went straight over to the window and examined it carefully without touching it. Then he looked down to see if he could possibly identify the spot where she had fallen, but it was too dark now, and he could distinguish no details at all. As he stood there straining his eyes he remembered her words during their conversation the day before— was it really no longer ago? ". . . I suppose you know what an ancestral precipice is, Inspector . . . some did it themselves —others were given help when they asked for it . . . others without asking for it . . . I wonder if anyone would want to give me help . . . without my asking for it . . ."

Had Miss Lethander had her suspicions? Although she had had the key on her when she fell down the precipice, which pointed to an accident—or suicide—the questions still pressed in on him. It struck him that this was in many respects an exact replica of Stella's death. She had fallen. Had *that* been an accident or a suicide? *She* hadn't been found until the day after. If the cat had not been heard miaowing, Miss Lethander's body would probably not have been found until the morning at the earliest, when they had begun to miss her. And in Stella's case the window had also been banging back and forth. Or had it? He couldn't remember whether Miss

Lethander had told him that or not, but that was of minor importance.

Durell was annoyed that they had immediately carried her up from the ravine. They could easily have established that she was dead and then summoned him, Durell. They knew he was in the house. They should know that, in a case like this, looking but not touching was the rule. It never did any harm for an experienced policeman to make his observations when it came to unexpected sudden death. His trained eye could reveal a great deal. Had she fallen forward or backward, done a swan dive, or plunged down headfirst or jumped a long way out, perhaps? And how was the body lying after the fall? And what were the injuries like in relation to position and objects on the ground? Loose stones, chunks of moss, sticks, and god knows what else could help give a picture of what had gone before and how it had happened.

He gave the window another close examination before closing it, unable to find footprints even under the magnifying glass, which would have been the case had she gotten up on the sill and thrown herself out. On the other hand, there was hardly a speck of dust, either. So there was nothing to show that Miss Lethander had not committed suicide. Nor was there any evidence to show that she had. What about an accident? Only his routine thoroughness and habit of testing out as many alternatives as possible made him even give that a thought. He could accept an accident theory only if, for instance, Miss Lethander had been cleaning the windows, or fiddling with the curtain rod, or something similar, and that he found hardly believable. He remembered what she had looked like as she had stood there by the window, a small blue shadow, her shoulders hardly reaching the windowsill. An accident from floor level was out of the question. As Durell went on thinking, a third alternative began to take firmer shape, in spite of the fact that he personally had made the key discovery that argued against it, and argued for the fact that she had locked herself in and, as far as could be seen, had been alone when this had happened. No, he could not abandon the alternative of murder. The key was very old and very unusual, but there *might* be copies. He sighed. Another murder. Behind another locked door. Not very opportune for someone trying to clear up the other two, and whether in that case there was a connection with the others was not exactly a question he could ignore. Naturally, thought Durell. But there were in fact two alternatives. Either there was a connection. Or there wasn't. Whether it was murder. And neither accident nor suicide.

He decided to phone Melander and his team that very evening, and in order not to spoil anything an investigator might like to find intact, he left the room tracing his own footsteps from the window to the door, then locked the door carefully behind him. In the absence of sealing materials, he took a toothpick out of his top pocket and manipulated it cunningly so that it would immediately reveal if someone tried to force the door in the interval before his colleagues arrived. But he was not particularly worried on that score, because if something the murderer had wanted had been in Miss Lethander's room or among her belongings, it was hardly likely to be there any longer.

24

MALIN

MALIN WAS STANDING WITH THE OTHERS DOWN IN THE HALL when the ambulance came, its headlights pointing straight at the open front door as it drove in between the gateposts. It swung around and stopped just below the steps. As they carried the old lady out Durell felt strongly that she was leaving little grief or regret behind her. His own sympathy for Miss Lethander was perhaps greater than anyone else's, but was also untainted by the pleasure of expectation. Hope they'll be disappointed in the end, he thought.

He stayed where he was while they escorted the stretcher to the back of the ambulance. They appeared to be making sure that the delicate little figure under the gray blanket was not going to play any more tricks, while maintaining a certain semblance of solemnity and grief as the vehicle finally drove away. There were no sirens to create a sense that there was life and hope, but silently and softly as Charon's ferry, it vanished into the darkness and disappeared in a halo of its own headlights.

Not until then did he notice the small, furtive glances between one person and another, and even a couple of suppressed smiles, though to be truthful, he saw it was the older generation who had to make an effort to satisfy the demands of convention.

He sought out Vera. She was slumped in an armchair with the cat on her lap—sitting there in silence, staring into space. He also saw that Alma—Miss Gren, the faithful retainer—had remained by the front door, gazing out into the darkness. She appeared to be deeply shaken, almost catatonic, until she suddenly straightened up, drew a deep breath, and disappeared toward the kitchen, or perhaps her room. He also saw Malin Rosceff, tall, coolly beautiful, slowly walking toward him. She stopped and hesitated.

"I was watching you, Inspector," she said. "I can understand that you find it unpleasant that they're so indifferent. Not to say pleased. At least some of them. You haven't got a poker face."

"Maybe not," said Durell. "But you could be wrong, since you've never played poker with me. I liked Miss Lethander very much."

"So did I. And since I don't care much about the money, it all seems so unnecessary."

"Unnecessary?" said Durell.

"I mean—I've got a feeling she did it so as not to be a nuisance any longer. There were so many of them in such a hurry, so to speak. And then—after all this with Martin and Victor, she probably thought it all too much. For her, too. She loved her family, you see."

"I suppose that must be true. And you? So you think it was suicide, do you?"

He looked at her with curiosity and she looked back at him in surprise. "Yes."

"What if this was also murder?"

Malin gasped and tried to say something, but was unable to utter the words, so finally Durell took pity on her.

"I did say *if*," he said. "Anyhow, I've sent for my colleagues. They're coming out and will make a thorough investigation to determine which. And *if* it turns out to be murder, then it would have been committed"—he glanced at his watch—"about three hours ago."

In some confusion, she searched his face to see if he were perhaps lying to her, though she could not see why he would.

"Maybe you've got one after all," she said finally. "A poker face. But in that case I don't understand . . ." She stopped abruptly, then went on very quickly, in an almost staccato voice. "Three hours ago—roughly between five and five-thirty. I was in the upstairs hall then, looking at the books in the bookcase—to see if there was anything readable there . . . and I heard someone come up the stairs from the kitchen and along the corridor to Aunt Lethander's room—then go in . . . It was Fredrik Svensson. You don't think . . ." She didn't complete the sentence, but looked him up and down with a frightened expression on her face. With a certain sense of inferiority, he wished he could have been a tall, handsome man, but on the other hand, this unexpected piece of information filled him with a corresponding amount of satisfaction.

"Go in? Didn't he knock?" he asked. "Did he just walk in? Surely everyone always knocked?"

"I don't know if he did or not, but I saw him go in. If he did knock, he didn't wait for an answer."

"Did you happen to see when he came out again?"

"No. I took a book and came down here and sat in that reading chair." She pointed at the big wing armchair by the window at the far end of the hall, its back to them. He realized she could hardly have seen anything from it.

"He must have used the kitchen stairs," she went on, "because otherwise I'd have heard him. He didn't come down these stairs, I'm sure."

"Could he have gone back to his room? That's up there, isn't it? At the end."

She laughed apologetically. "I'm afraid I don't know which room he and his wife have been given. But I know he uses the kitchen stairs for various purposes. But—to answer your question—of course he might have gone back to his room without my noticing."

"How long were you down here?"

"Not long. I took the book with me and went back to our room—when would that be?—a quarter of an hour later, perhaps. I don't know if Fredrik was still up there then."

"No, of course not, how could you know that?"

Durell gazed at her with his pale-blue blank expression, the gaze he considered his poker gaze, which she showed no sign of taking the same way, so he went on. "Then I must ask him. Thank you for the information, Mrs. Rosceff. I don't think Fredrik Svensson would have volunteered it himself."

25

FREDRIK

THEN THE HOUSE WAS ONCE AGAIN FULL OF POLICEMEN AND their equipment. Durell gave them a quick briefing before taking them up to Miss Lethander's room. First he made sure the toothpick had not been disturbed, then he unlocked the door and let them in. He put the key in Melander's hand, then suddenly remembered the roll of film from the forest. He fished it out of his pocket and handed it over.

"Can you get this off to the lab?" he said. "I almost forgot it in the confusion."

He walked back along the corridor, through the dining room, then the hall, past Martin's and Victor's rooms, continuing along the whole length of the house until he came to the room occupied by the Svenssons.

Fredrik Svensson opened the door, his face quite flushed, his shirt unbuttoned far down his hairy chest. His belt was slung below his stomach and he made no effort to keep his belly and chest in line. He reeked of whiskey. On the table over by the window, where his wife was sitting with her hands nervously fluttering in her lap, her eyes fixed on Durell, was a highly prized bottle of whiskey.

"Well, look who's here," he said. He stepped aside and with a swing of his large, flabby hand, he invited Durell to come in.

"And what can I do for you? Some whiskey, perhaps?" Durell shook his head, gazing around the room and stopping at Ulla.

"You see," Fredrik went, "I thought we could do with a little pick-me-up after all that fuss, so I commandeered that bottle, because if I hadn't, someone else would have pretty quick. A small advance on my inheritance, you might say."

He closed the door behind him with what sounded like a pleased titter. Ulla, clearly embarrassed and upset by his behavior as well as by Durell's presence, flushed slowly from the neck upward and avoided Durell's eyes.

"What were you doing in Miss Lethander's room this afternoon?" said Durell quietly.

Fredrik screwed up his eyes and looked craftily at him.

"So you say I was in the old girl's room this afternoon. Why do you say that?"

"I didn't say it. I asked what you were doing there?"

Ulla sat up.

"Did you go and see her after all, Fredrik?" she said. "We agreed—"

"Be quiet," he snapped. "Yes, I went to her room to talk some sense into her about the loan. You said you were going to rest. I thought I could manage on my own, and don't you think I was afraid to talk it out with the old girl."

Durell interrupted him.

"Yes, Mr. Svensson. So you were going to see old Miss Lethander and ask her for a small temporary loan. Is that right?"

"Temporary loan? No, much more than that."

The big burly man in front of him nodded sulkily, his chin and cheeks wobbling as he did so. It was not hard for Durell to see that this man was quick tempered, and that if he asked for anything and was refused, especially if he'd reinforced himself beforehand, then he was capable of anything.

"I had it out with her the other evening. I suppose I wasn't very diplomatic then, and she was angry, refusing even to discuss the matter. But then I thought the time had come for another shot—after what had happened to Martin and Victor, I mean, she'd be a bit softer, I thought. You'd think it'd make her be a bit more considerate toward her family—*our* family, too, I mean."

"So you had a talk with her?"

"No. That is, I went in. But I didn't talk to her."

"Why not?"

"Because she wasn't there. Just imagine, after I'd at last made the decision, the old girl simply wasn't there."

Durell tried a new angle of approach. "You left your wife here, if I've got it right, and she didn't know you were going to talk to Miss Lethander about a loan, because if she'd known your plans, she would've wanted to come with you. But you didn't want that. I find it hard to see what *reason* you had for not letting her go with you. Didn't the old lady like your wife?"

"Oh, yes. She liked Ulla better than me, but that wasn't the point. The question was that I'd have to be a bit firmer to get her to see reason, and that wouldn't have worked if Ulla'd been there. I mean, she'd have started blubbering and making a fuss and all that. That sort of thing doesn't suit Fredrik Svensson."

"I see. Tell me—you went up the kitchen stairs. Was that so that you wouldn't be seen?"

Fredrik looked away and did not answer immediately.

"I was in the pantry," he said finally. "Getting myself a little booster—a snort, you might say."

Ulla nodded eagerly.

"That's what he said he was going to do when he left, but I had no idea he was going to see her afterward," she said.

"And when you'd had your snort, you went on up the kitchen stairs, knocked on Miss Lethander's door, went into the room, and she wasn't there, you say."

"That's right."

"So you just walked in. Without knocking? But you must have knocked on the door first?"

Fredrik looked uncertain, but then nodded firmly. "I knocked on the door."

"And then although she wasn't there, and you couldn't have heard her telling you to come in, you opened the door and walked in? Wasn't that a bit crude, Mr. Svensson? Considering what you had gone there for, and you were trying not to annoy her?"

"Isn't a knock enough?" he asked. "Do you have to wait for a reply, too? I think that's going too far. Anyhow, I went in—the door wasn't locked. If she'd wanted to be left alone, she'd have locked the door, wouldn't she? She usually did."

"So you went in. What did you do then?"

Fredrik gestured vaguely with his hands. "Do then? I looked around, of course. I looked into her bedroom. The door was open a little, so it was tempting to take a peek into a millionairess's boudoir, if you see what I mean."

"Supposing she'd been in there?" said Durell. "That would've looked bad, wouldn't it?"

"If she'd been in there, the door would've been closed, wouldn't it? You can be sure of that." He paused. "Won't you change your mind and have a snort?"

"No, thank you. But think carefully now, Mr. Svensson. Was the window open when you went in?"

Fredrik walked over to the table and filled his glass. He seemed to be trying to remember, his forehead creasing with the effort.

"I don't know," he said finally. "Never gave it a thought. An open window isn't very remarkable, is it? You just don't think about it. Anyhow, *I* didn't open any window."

Ulla suddenly broke into the conversation. "Aunt Lethander always used to sleep with her window open, and it's likely the window was open because she liked fresh air."

"Yes, that's true, now that you mention it," said Fredrik, the heavy frown vanishing. "I think the window may have been open. She usually had it open for her little after-noon nap."

"And the bedroom door was shut," said Durell. "And then —when you couldn't find her—what did you do?"

"I came back here, of course. Ulla was asleep. For once she managed to sleep without any of those damned pills."

"So you didn't try to find Miss Lethander? You came straight back here?"

Fredrik sighed. "No, I made a detour."

"A detour? You mean you went via the pantry? I see."

Durell looked at him, then went on. "Do you know if anyone saw you go into Miss Lethander's room?"

Fredrik smiled slightly. "I'd worked that one out. I suppose someone did. Why else would you have come here, and why would you start asking me what I was *doing* in there? I'm not that stupid."

"So because you've worked it out that someone saw you, you're prepared to admit you were there. Not even your wife knew about it."

Fredrik was looking at him in a different way now, Durell thought, his liverish eyes more blurred.

"I told you the truth, anyhow, whoever saw me, or didn't see me."

"Of course," said Durell dryly. "But maybe you're not telling me the whole truth. *If*, for instance, Miss Lethander had actually been there, and if you'd started talking to her about this loan, and if she'd refused you immediately, then you may well have lost your head and grabbed the old girl and simply chucked her out the window. It was open—so it wouldn't be difficult. And that would also have been a way of extracting a little more money in the not-too-distant future."

As Durell presented his vision of what might have happened Fredrik's face slowly turned scarlet, and he started breathing heavily. Ulla rose to her feet. For a few seconds she stood as if paralyzed, staring at him, and Durell came to the conclusion that as far as her experience with her husband went, the course of events Durell had described was quite plausible.

She and Fredrik looked into each other's eyes and he slowly started shaking his big head. Then he grabbed the bottle, filled his glass to the top, and sank down in the chair opposite her.

"Ulla," he said in a thick voice, "you can't believe that. Even if—even if it had been like that, I'd never have thrown her out the window. Christ, you both heard that I could hardly remember whether the window was open."

He looked around beseechingly, and Durell couldn't help smiling slightly at such amazing logic.

"I might have hit her," Fredrik went on. "No, no, not even that. Not a defenseless old thing like that—not if I hadn't thought it out beforehand—er—that the old girl would be better off dead. And what would be the point of that if I wanted to borrow money from her—because I wanted the money then and there, quickly."

He looked beseechingly at Ulla. "Tell me you don't believe all that. Then I'll admit I took all your sleeping pills and chucked them down the toilet."

Durell studied the scene before him with a slight sense of guilt over the agonies he had aroused with his speculations, but also with considerable interest. Reactions were always interesting, and although it was not always considered particularly ethical to provoke them, they were no less interesting for all that. Then he noticed that Ulla's face was flushed for the second time during his visit.

"Let me say something," she said suddenly. "If Fredrik went in and Aunt Lethander wasn't there, and the window was open, couldn't that mean that she had already—that she was already lying down in the ravine?"

Durell shook his head. "Fredrik maintains that the door was open when he went in. But it was locked when Miss Lethander was found, and she had the key in her pocket. *If* she was already down there, then we do know *one* thing. Miss

Lethander did not commit suicide. She was murdered. And if there's no other key to the door to her room, then the murderer must have had an opportunity to put the key in her pocket before I had an opportunity to examine her."

Durell was not sure they had followed his reasoning, but he studied the effect carefully, all the same. There was a long silence—that was all. He hunched his shoulders slightly and started walking up and down the room between the table and the door, keeping to the narrow lines in the pattern along the edge of the carpet, talking all the time.

"So it must have been like that, with one important prerequisite—and that is that she really *was* down there in the ravine when Mr. Fredrik Svensson went in to borrow some money. If she were not, then it's possible she committed suicide. Now try to remember, Fredrik Svensson. Did you notice whether the window was locked or not?"

Fredrik shook his head, his cheeks trembling again, but the high color in his face had gone.

"And when you looked into the bedroom, are you sure no one was there?"

Fredrik shook his head and almost whispered his reply. "I don't think so. I didn't notice anything. But the door was only slightly ajar, so . . ."

". . . someone *might* have been in there without your seeing?"

Ulla had leaned back in her chair, but when Durell said that, she sat up again and spoke one single word.

"Alma."

Then she told them about the sleeping pill she had gone to borrow from Miss Lethander, about the voices she had heard, one of them Miss Lethander's, the other Alma's, and that all this had happened a quarter of an hour or so before Fredrik had gone to see the old lady. And finally—finally she told them that her son, who liked running in the forest, had witnessed a quarrel between Miss Lethander and Alma when they were out on their daily walk after lunch. And that

Charles had heard Alma say to Miss Lethander, "You can be sure I'll stop you at any price . . ." When she stopped talking, Durell looked thoughtfully at her for a long time, unable to resist wondering what it could have been Alma had wanted to stop.

26

ALMA

HE FOUND HER IN THE KITCHEN. HE STOPPED JUST INSIDE THE door and cleared his throat to catch her attention, for she was sitting there, apparently scarcely aware of his presence, her bare-armed plump body completely hiding the chair she was sitting on. When she finally raised her eyes, he spoke to her.

"Miss Gren," he said, "I'm very sorry to have to bother you again. But it's about the death of Miss Lethander."

She nodded, gesturing toward the kitchen bench, but he chose to pretend not to have noticed, as a certain distance gave him a better chance of observing her.

"When I met you upstairs today—before . . . the accident . . . you were coming from Miss Lethander's room, weren't you?"

"Yes," she said, looking at him, a question in her eyes. "The accident? So you know it was an accident?"

"Don't you think it was?"

"No."

"So you think it was suicide?"

She nodded slowly, but did not reply.

"Let's not get involved in what it might have been at the moment," he said. "But I'd like to ask you a few questions. First of all, you and Miss Lethander were very close to each other, weren't you?"

"What do you mean? I've lived in this house for over forty years and done just about everything. There used to be three people working here, but times have changed. If by being close to her you mean that I've become a friend and confidante to Miss Lethander over all these years, then you're right. And at this moment—now—well, Inspector, I *can* control myself. But I feel a terrible loss, and terrible grief."

"I'm sure you do," Durell said, then paused. "But there was a great difference in age between you, wasn't there?"

"Maybe so, but I never felt it. Miss Lethander was a very unusual person. She didn't find it easy to adapt to newfangled ideas, and yet she kept up with things. And she was always herself. She could afford to be herself. Live as she liked."

Durell noted that a very small, sorrowful smile had suddenly appeared in Alma's eyes.

"And die as she liked?" he said.

Alma Gren turned to look at him.

"What do you mean?" she said.

"I mean, if she'd fallen ill? How would you have managed? Was there ever any suggestion of moving from here? To a relative's or to an old people's home? This is a large house. You'd never have been able to manage everything if she'd fallen ill, would you?"

"It was never mentioned."

"But what about you? What would you have done?"

"If she'd decided to move? I've never given the matter a thought."

Durell tried to make himself even clearer. "I mean . . . if Miss Lethander had decided to sell the house and move in with one of her relatives, what would have happened to you?"

"Miss Lethander had already arranged for that. But the question never arose. If she had gone . . . we talked about it once . . . she'd arranged for me in her will, she said. And, anyhow, I've saved quite a bit myself, I'll have you know, and I'll be getting my pension soon. I'll manage all right."

She met Durell's eyes with a certain chilliness, implying

she did not like him to talk like this about her affairs. But Durell pretended not to notice.

"Was Miss Lethander often ill?" he said.

"No, not at all. On the contrary. She was extremely healthy. We went for a walk every day because she thought that was good for her. Only a few hours before . . . well, we went for our walk today, too. And then she always had a nap. The walk made her sleep better, she said."

"So she found it difficult to sleep otherwise, you mean?"

"Not exactly difficult. But she took sleeping pills. She used to take one every night. Perhaps she found it hard to go to sleep at night, when she'd already had a nap in the daytime."

"I see. Tell me, Miss Gren. Those sleeping pills—did she keep them in her bedroom?"

"No. I used to take one up to her every evening. I used to give it to her after she'd woken up after her walk, so that I wouldn't have to disturb her later on."

"Later on?" Durell frowned. "But you said earlier today, Miss Gren, that Miss Lethander had French habits, as you expressed it. You dined late. Wouldn't that be a more appropriate time to give her the pill, in that case?"

Miss Gren's voice was noticeably dry when she answered him. "As soon as I clear the dinner table, I go to bed. Miss Lethander often stayed up reading in the upstairs hall. That sleeping-pill routine had become a habit."

"And what about today? When did you take it up today?"

"After our walk, as usual—after she'd woken up."

"But, Miss Gren, the pill you took up—as I see it, Miss Lethander gave that to Ulla Svensson. Isn't that so? She knocked on the door and asked for a sleeping pill and was given one. She also told me, by the way, that *you* were there then. That's right, is it?"

She looked suspiciously at him.

"Yes," she said. "That's right. But I don't see what you're getting at."

"Well, since Ulla Svensson was given that pill, presumably

Miss Lethander wanted another one. Didn't she? So maybe you went down to get her another one?"

Alma Gren looked troubled, and Durell watched to see what would happen to that reaction, but it floated away into space and she answered him quite calmly. "Well, I did actually mean to, but I forgot all about it for a while, because —well, perhaps I'm getting old. And I had already done it . . . I mean, she'd already been given her pill, so getting her another one was rather unusual. When I realized I'd forgotten it, I took up another one right away. That was when I met you, when you were going to talk to Miss Lethander, and I told you she probably wanted to be left in peace, because she hadn't answered my knock. Surely you remember all that."

"Yes, of course I do, Miss Gren. The door was locked then?"

"Yes."

"So you also tried the door to see if it was locked?"

"Yes."

The silence between them grew as his thoughts wandered.

"Wasn't Miss Lethander afraid of being behind locked doors?" he said finally. "Generally speaking, I mean. If anything happened to her, you wouldn't be able to get in and help. Do you see what I mean?"

"Yes, I see what you mean." She paused briefly. "But I've got my own key to Miss Lethander's room. I keep it in my room."

Durell felt something leap inside him.

"You've got a key?" he said tensely.

"Yes, I keep it safe in my sewing table. Miss Lethander gave express orders that I wasn't to use the key unless I really thought something had happened to her. She once said, 'If I should break my leg, or have a stroke, or something like that—I promise you I'll scream as loudly as I can, and then you can use that key. But otherwise, you'll know that *if* my door's locked, I don't want to be disturbed.' "

"Are you sure that key's in your sewing table now?"

"Absolutely certain. I saw it this morning, and I saw it a few hours ago, and no one knows where I keep it. Not even Miss Lethander knew."

Durell's thoughts whirled, associations rising at a furious speed and questions piling up to be answered. But he knew she could see nothing of that. He knew the game well enough to use his poker face when necessary. He put his fingertips together and said, "Where are the sleeping pills?"

"In the pantry."

She got up, went over to the pantry door, opened it, and reached up to one of the shelves inside. Then she came back and placed a small glass bottle in front of Durell.

"Here they are," she said.

Durell picked up the bottle and shook it, then smiled at Alma.

"There are quite a few left," he said. "Did Miss Lethander know where this bottle was kept?"

"Of course. Of course she did."

He nodded with satisfaction, then he suddenly swung around and said rather more harshly then he had meant to, "Miss Gren, you assume old Miss Lethander committed suicide, don't you?"

"What do you mean?"

"You believe she threw herself out of the window down the ancestral precipice. How can you believe she chose that method when she had a whole pantryful of sleeping pills? No—Miss Gren—you can't convince *me* of that, anyhow. Nor that you believe it yourself for one single moment. Miss Lethander was murdered—thrown down there—the door locked—who locked the door? Miss Gren—answer me now—did you murder old Miss Lethander?"

She was as white as a sheet as she rose from her chair and almost reeled back at his furious accusation. But she collected herself swiftly, lowered her hands, then started walking up and down the room. "Oh, dear lord, dear lord, how *can* you believe that?"

Then Durell dropped his bombshell. "I know you threatened Miss Lethander during your walk on Saturday and I can tell you how she died."

Alma stopped and stared at him, her face scarlet, her eyes open wide, and her mouth gasping with dismay. Durell went on without taking his eyes off her.

"You'd crossed swords with her. Or the other way around, perhaps. She'd decided to move from this house, and for you that meant you would lose your home. You quarreled about it, and she threatened to cut you out of her will. And you? You decided to kill her. Today, when you were up with her the first time—with the first sleeping pill—you quarreled about it again. You tried to get her to change her mind, but she was stubborn. Ulla Svensson heard *that* quarrel. And then"—he made a calculated pause—"the *second* time you went up—with the *second* pill—you also had the key with you. And when it was all over . . ." He looked at her appraisingly. "You're physically a very strong woman, Miss Gren. When it was all over, you suddenly heard someone knocking on the door. What did you do then? Hide, perhaps? In the bedroom. Miss Lethander's bedroom. But as soon as the coast was clear, you slipped out and locked the door behind you, then went down to your room and put the key back."

He fell silent. She said nothing, hunched over the table, her head on her arms, her whole body shaking with sobs.

Durell went on, an inexpressible gentleness in his voice. "Was it like that? Tell me if it wasn't."

A long time passed before the convulsions in that heavy body stopped and she straightened up to meet his eyes again.

"Why are you saying all this?" she said.

"Why did you quarrel with her on your walk on Saturday? Why did you quarrel with her today? What did you mean when you said she could be quite sure you'd stop her at any price?" He paused. "Disinheriting you, maybe? Moving out of the house?"

She had no time to reply because at that moment Melander

came into the kitchen and thrust a photograph at Durell.

"The film was unexposed except for one frame. This must be the last taken with that camera by *that* photographer. Sorry to disturb you . . ."

He departed as quickly as he had come. Durell spent a long time looking at the photograph and once again the mists and darkness descended. He sighed.

"Or did you mean stop her from killing Victor and Martin?"

Without a word, he gave her the photograph.

It was of Victor's room, the table in the foreground, a gun lying on top of it, and farther away, by the door, old Miss Lethander holding her hand up in a threatening gesture.

Alma looked at it for a long time, then shook her head.

"No, no," she said. "Our quarrel—Miss Lethander told me she was going to do just what I thought she'd done today—kill herself. She thought that at last the time had come for her to fulfill the expectations of the people all around her. *She* had nothing to do with the deaths of Victor and Martin."

"And yet we don't know," said Durell gravely. "But what we do know is that Miss Lethander was also murdered, and that murderer is here, right in the middle of us all."

27

VERONICA

THE SUN SHINING STRAIGHT THROUGH THE WINDOW INTO MY eyes woke me up, and I wondered vaguely why the curtains had been drawn back. I had slept very badly that night. Everything that had happened the day before, and of course the days before that, kept swirling around in my head, the same images over and over again, the same thoughts, making me feel as if I were floating somewhere between dream and reality. Sometimes I found myself wide awake, sitting straight up in bed wondering where I was. Then, when I remembered, it all became almost more unreal than the unreality I had dreamed about. When I lay back on the pillow again and tried to go to sleep, listening to Vera's calm breathing from the bed on the other side, I was surprised and confused that she could take it all so calmly, sleeping undisturbed as if nothing had happened.

I opened my eyes and looked over at her bed. It was empty. The bed was made, although she hadn't bothered to put on the blanket that served as a bedspread. So I realized it was Vera who had sabotaged the only peaceful sleep I'd had by letting in the sunlight. At first I thought she was in the bathroom, but there was no sound from there, so I figured she'd already gone out.

I got out of bed, went over to the window, and drew the

curtains across again before taking off my nightgown and going into the bathroom, because the Yugoslav might have been sitting over there looking straight in at me, and I wasn't going to provide him with that entertainment. Just as I was about to turn on the shower I heard Ellen's voice through the wall. "No, I'm not staying any longer. I don't care what happens, I'm going back to the manor, and I think you should come with me . . ." Then Vera's voice. "Not me. I'm staying, especially now, to see how things develop. You can take Veronica with you, then you won't have to be alone . . ."

It was disagreeable hearing almost every word so clearly between the bathroom and Ellen's room, as clearly as if there'd been no wall at all—almost like spying on them—so I turned on the shower with pleasure, since the noise silenced them. I wondered if Vera was staying because of the inspector. I would have had no objection to leaving. I wouldn't have minded going to the manor if Ellen wanted me to, but I'd have preferred to go back to Stockholm and my boutique and normality. Then it struck me that that was unthinkable before Martin's and Victor's and Aunt Lethander's . . . I really couldn't think about it. I didn't want to think about it. I could feel myself beginning to cry, and I turned my face up into the shower so I wouldn't know whether it was water or tears pouring down my face.

After breakfast I went out and sat on the steps of the big house. Charlene, Charlotte and John's little girl, was already there, sitting on the top step, with a large cup of soapy water and a paper tube someone had made for her out of a page from a magazine. The remains of the magazine and some more tubes lay beside her. Those miserly Svenssons, I thought—couldn't even give the child proper toys. Then it struck me that perhaps it wasn't all that easy to get hold of such things, and that this marvelous morning was made for a little girl wanting to blow bubbles. She was really clever at it, but couldn't make particularly large bubbles. As I sat there I kept wanting to try it myself. "May I try a tube?" I said.

"May I try, too?" She went on blowing, but at the same time kept looking encouragingly at me.

It was great fun. We competed at making the largest and loveliest bubbles, and when we let them go and they sailed upward like shimmering, trembling balloons, we both laughed, and when they burst we both said . . . ooooh, what a shame. Then we blew some more, and laughed and got along really well. I tore out some more pages and rolled some more tubes, dismayed to find the soapy water disappearing so fast.

Naturally I saw the police car coming, but I didn't really notice, since that had happened so many times during the last few days, and the presence of the police out here had become so ordinary. Charlene didn't pay much attention, either. She went on blowing bubbles. So I went on dipping the tube into the soapy water, making a special effort to create a masterpiece. The thin membrane of soap and water expanded and expanded, trembling agitatedly on the end of the tube, while I concentrated on watching—blowing calmly and evenly and carefully. I could see Charlene out of the corner of my eye, watching the growing miracle, her mouth wide open and following the creation of what might be the largest and most beautiful and most rainbowlike bubble of them all, and when I felt my masterpiece was complete, I made the soft movement with my hand that soap-bubble conductors always make when their creation is to be released from its umbilical cord. The bubble hung in the air in front of me for a few seconds, as large as a football, handsome in its harmonious airiness, then slowly began to rise, hesitantly, trembling like a cello vibrato. I watched it.

"A veritable work of art," I heard, and then, "Isn't it?"

I knew at once who it was, but I hadn't noticed him coming. As I answered I glanced at him. He was standing there looking entranced, staring at the rising bubble. He appeared quite detached—as if listening to something as he watched, his pale blue eyes blank, and not returning to reality until the bubble suddenly burst in a shower of microscopic drops.

"But, oh, so transitory," he added dryly.

He looked at me thoughtfully for a while, and just as I was going to say something about ordinary soapy water and a paper tube actually making the best bubbles by far because the paper absorbed the water so well, he said something that at once confused and bewildered me.

"Thank you, Veronica. That was one of the best demonstrations I've had for a long time." He paused, still looking straight at me. Then he went on. "Do you mind if we have a little talk over there in a few minutes? I just have to ask one of my men to do something for me."

We sat down by the garden table. I was terribly nervous about what he wanted to talk to me about because he'd sent the police car away, which I thought was very significant. He looked at me in a friendly way, no doubt aware of the state I was in.

"It's about old Miss Lethander," he said. "When you saw her down there in the ravine, you shouted for help, didn't you?"

"I don't know," I said. "I just screamed, I'm afraid. I'm sure you think I'm a real drip, bawling away every time something happens. But I'm not. It's just that right now it seems to me the horrors will never come to an end."

"Yes, you could say that. But when you screamed—people came rushing up at once, didn't they?"

"Yes, of course. Thank goodness they did, because I couldn't move. I was paralyzed. And that cat down there—it was like something supernatural."

"Cats wail and dogs howl on their masters' graves. You've heard that, I suppose. But you didn't let the body out of your sight, did you? You could see her all the time?"

"Yes, I told you. I was standing there, paralyzed."

"And then—what happened then?"

"They came, of course. Carl was first, I think—then the Yugoslav. They jumped over the fence and climbed down, then carried her up and put her down here on the lawn.

Then the others came. I don't know how long I went on screaming—yes, I do—it felt good when the boys came, Carl and the other one."

"She was lying on a blanket. When I arrived she was lying on a blanket. Do you know who got hold of that blanket?"

I shook my head, trying to remember.

"A moss-green blanket, with gray stripes—didn't you notice the blanket?"

"Yes, of course I saw it, but I didn't think about what it looked like."

Although I was feeling under pressure from all his questions, it suddenly occurred to me that of course I could tell him whose blanket it was—moss green with gray stripes. I even remembered I had noticed it and had thought about it as it lay there spread out on the lawn.

"It was Vera's blanket—or, rather, it was the blanket that was used as a bedspread on her bed," I said.

"Are there any other blankets like it in the house?"

"I don't know. But when I woke up this morning—when she'd gone to see Ellen, I mean . . ." I stopped and felt confused again because I remembered Vera's bedspread hadn't been on the bed when I woke up, although she'd made the bed.

"This morning, I noticed," I went on, "that the blanket wasn't in our room. I don't know if there are any more like it."

"I see. Did Vera put the blanket down on the lawn?"

"I don't know. I really don't. There were so many people there—Ellen and Malin and Vera and Mauritz and . . . What are you getting at, anyway?"

He looked at me and shook his head. "At the truth. Whatever it looks like."

We sat in silence for a long time, as if one of us were waiting for the other to say something. He was the one to speak first, and his question frightened me. "Vera didn't like her father, did she?"

"No."

"Or her brother?"

"No."

"Or old Miss Lethander?"

I couldn't stand it any longer. I got up feeling very disturbed, and it was only with a huge effort that I could keep my voice steady.

"I don't know," I said. "But for god's sake, tell me what you're getting at. You say at the truth. What have all these questions got to do with that? Vera has nothing to do with all this. Are you . . ." I could feel I was getting very agitated. "Are you crazy?"

He smiled, as if he had wanted to ask that question himself, but he went on, disregarding my feelings.

"Do you know where Vera was after the party last Saturday?"

"No, I don't. I went to bed about midnight, and since I was so tired, I fell asleep just like that."

"Didn't you notice whether she came in or not? Or *when* she came in? Or *what* she was doing? Or when she went to bed, or anything else that happened?"

"No."

His monotonous obstinacy made me want to cry. I felt like screaming again, and just leaving everything.

"Good," he said gently.

I looked at him, astounded to find how upset I had been a moment earlier. He looked back, his lips curled sadly.

"I mean," he said, "you don't have to tell me or anyone else *whether* you noticed when she came and went, or *whether* you noticed she was doing anything, or *whether* she wasn't in your room during the night. When it comes to statements, it is, in spite of everything, the *next* best."

He sighed and got up.

"Thank you, Veronica," he said. Then he left. He walked beneath an apple tree and reached up for an apple, but couldn't reach it. He made a few feeble attempts, but then I

suppose he realized how foolish he must look, so he turned
around and smiled apologetically.

"You see?" he said. "I'm not exactly built for stealing
apples."

The police car was away for about an hour, and as soon as
it returned, this time with Melander and two more policemen in it as well, the inspector disappeared into the house
with them all in his wake, just like a hospital doctor on his
rounds with his attendants behind him. I knew something
was up. At that moment Vera came out of Ellen's room. She
came up to me and said, taking the words right out of my
mouth, "Let's join in. Something's up, I'm sure."

We went into the hall. We turned out not to have been
alone in noticing the new police invasion. Most of them were
there—John Bokström and Ulla with Charlene in her arms,
Fredrik and Carl and Gittan and Charles. Malin and her
Yugoslav appeared from the kitchen, he still with an open
sandwich in his hand, and even though he didn't understand
a word we were saying—or, rather, whispering, because that
was the mood of the moment—he nevertheless seemed equally
interested. He asked Malin questions and she answered him.
I noticed with some admiration that she spoke Serbo-
Croatian fluently. Mauritz and Charlotte were the only ones
missing.

We were standing in the hall looking up the stairs when
suddenly the inspector appeared, looking like a modern
Napoleon, his red hair seemingly against the white ceiling
and the great crystal chandelier, and he actually had his hand
thrust inside his blue-striped jacket. He raised his other hand
to catch our attention.

"We're going to do a brief reconstruction," he said.

I was surprised by the sharp authority in his voice, which
sounded different from that of our earlier conversation. It
was sonorous and full now. He looked more like an actor on
the stage or an opera singer about to launch into his first note.

"You will hear shots up here," he went on. "But don't let

it worry you—nothing will happen. But we'd like some of you to assist us."

He let his gaze sweep over all of us and suddenly said, "Where is Mrs. Bokström?"

"In our room," said John. He sounded nervous.

"Good. One of my men will come down now and go with you to your room. You are to stay there until we ask you to come back here again. Where is Miss Gren?"

"In the kitchen."

Malin had answered, as loudly and distinctly as the inspector himself, and I noticed him smiling, because he realized she was actually imitating him. Vera nudged me and whispered, "God, the man's got a sense of humor as well."

Then he went on. "Good. One of our men will now come down, and I'd be grateful, Mrs. Rosceff, if you would show him to wherever Miss Gren is, and then stay there in her room until we ask you to come back here again." He paused deliberately.

"Our men will give you further instructions," he added.

There was another brief pause before he went on again. "Mr. Svensson—would you and your wife please come up here and, with Mr. Melander here, go to Miss Lethander's room? Would you then please stay there until we ask you to come back here again? If you don't mind."

Two policemen came swiftly down the stairs, and with a bewildered-looking John, who had dark patches of sweat under his armpits, and Malin, now looking absorbed by the significance of the moment, they went off along the kitchen corridor. I saw John and his attendants vanish into their room, and a confused-looking Alma being fetched out of the kitchen by the others, taken into her own room, and the door closing behind them. At the same time, Fredrik and Ulla started up the stairs. For once, Fredrik was quite sober, even pale. Ulla still had Charlene with her, and before they were halfway up, the poor child started whining, then screaming. Then what was almost a miracle happened. Durell let his left hand glance off her cheek and the scream died away into a contented sigh. Vera whispered into my ear, "God, he's good with kids, too."

Now that the arrangement was complete, our diminutive Napoleon continued.

"Vera and Veronica Bernheim, would you please come up here with me? And you others, please sit anywhere you like . . . and . . . many thanks for your attention."

He suddenly pulled his hand out from its hiding place inside his jacket, and a shiver went through my whole body as I was on my way up the stairs, Vera beside me. He had a gun in his hand.

We stood in the middle of the upstairs hall outside Martin's and Victor's rooms. I noticed the seals had been removed. Durell seemed to have forgotten our existence. He went into Victor's room and closed the door. Then we heard a shot. It didn't sound particularly horrible, but I closed my eyes all the same and clung to Vera's arm because I realized that this was deadly serious—that was when he had died—his brown hair falling over his forehead for the last time, the slightly insolent, superior smile in his eyes stiffening in surprise, and all that spoiled willfulness ebbing away into nothing. And although I knew Vera found it difficult to understand his way of life, I sensed that she was feeling the same as I was. Then Durell came out again. He was still holding the pistol in his hand. Without even glancing at us, he opened the door to Martin's room and went inside. Before the door closed, I just managed to catch a glimpse of a faint glow in the fireplace—glowing embers after a fire has died down. I looked at Vera in surprise.

"Did you see the fire?" I said.

"Yes, I did," she said, nodding. "I asked Alma to lay a fire in there this morning."

"What for?"

"He telephoned and asked me to."

"Who?"

"Him." She nodded toward the closed door.

I don't know how long we waited, silent and tense, wondering what he was doing in there, the inspector. Then suddenly there was another shot, and he came out just as solemnly as when he had come out of Victor's room. He walked over to me.

"Would you get them now—those in Miss Lethander's room."

As I walked away I heard him calling down the stairs. "Would you get them now—those I asked to shut themselves away in their rooms."

A minute or so later, we were all back again, and he was standing up there against the white of the ceiling and the chandelier, but no longer with his hand inside his jacket.

"Thank you for your cooperation," he said. His voice was the same as before, sonorous, loud, imperative, but more tense now.

"Did you hear the shots?" he said. "Those of you who were in Mr. and Mrs. Bokström's room—did you hear the shots?"

"Yes, we heard both shots," replied the policeman.

"And those who were in Alma Gren's room—did you hear the shots?"

The other policeman replied, "Yes, we heard two shots."

"And those who were in Miss Lethander's room—did you hear the shots?"

"No," said Melander. "No, we didn't hear any shots."

Durell looked out over us, and I had a feeling that maybe what he said next was more than regulations permitted, or whatever it was that decided what you could and could not say in situations like this.

"So that alibi falls to pieces in your hands, my sweet . . ."

I happened to glance at Vera at that moment. She closed her eyes behind those large glasses of hers and turned terribly pale—and yet a smile was playing around her lips.

28

VERA

HE WAS ALONE WITH HER. THEY HAD RETREATED TO MISS
Lethander's room, and he was sitting in the same chair he
had sat in a few days earlier, when he had met the old lady
for the first time. Not without melancholy, he listened to the
ticking of the clock, saw the clear blue sky through the window, where she had stood and told him about the unchangeable that was constantly changing, and given him her caustic
opinion of life today.

But now Vera was standing there, not so small or so
ethereally delicate as old Miss Lethander, but not that much
taller, either. She was standing with her back to the wall,
looking at him very seriously, almost with fear. Strangely
enough, he didn't mind much about that. He had to do this.
He felt like a schoolboy after a math test who had to calm his
anxious curiosity and test his answers against those of his
friends, regardless of whether the result would be a disap-
pointment or a joy.

"You have to start from one standpoint," he said. "It's no
longer a matter of identifying but of identification. Everything will be so much easier for both of us if you'll cooperate.
Do you want to cooperate?"

She nodded so faintly he hardly saw it.

"So," he went on, "that evening Victor went into his room,

quite pleased with himself, I imagine. He sat down in the armchair by the table and put the gun down in front of him. We don't know how he got hold of it, but perhaps it's no more complicated than that he found it in your father's room and simply took it. Perhaps he wondered why Martin had brought it with him, but now that he had it in his room, it wasn't all that important. He picked up his camera and extracted the roll of film—oh, what a lot of fine photos on it. He'd no doubt make a pretty penny, and he'd also gotten some interesting additions to his own private album. He put the exposed film in his briefcase, took out a new roll, and put it in the camera. Just as he finished doing that there was a knock on the door.

"He opened the door. Outside was Miss Lethander. He asked her to come in, probably somewhat puzzled by such a late visit from an old lady, but nevertheless not so uneasy that he didn't rather disrespectfully sit down again to find out what she wanted. She was upset, or anyhow annoyed with him for taking his cousin's wife up to the attic. She had seen them slip up there from her sitting room and she told him nothing good would come of such behavior. 'Watch out, my boy—I've seen a great deal of evil come from that kind of lightheartedness.' "

He paused and stared at Vera.

"You're guessing," she said dryly.

"Yes, I'm guessing. Whether that was what happened or not doesn't matter. We'll come to the essentials in a moment. The next step, you see, is no longer simply a matter of guessing. Listen to me now. Old Miss Lethander retreated toward the door, and just as she was about to leave the room Victor picked up the camera and took a photograph. She was angry—he could see that—but he just laughed it off. After she left there was an interval, then another knock on the door. This time it was Charles, and the question is whether Victor did not suddenly have reason to reflect on what Aunt Lethander had said, because Charles was angry, and certainly not harmless. After a tense moment, Charles demanded the film of the photographs Victor had taken of his beautiful wife. To show that he meant what he was saying, Charles suddenly picked up the gun lying on the table and pointed it at Victor. It is possible Victor turned pale—because he probably knew the gun was loaded. But he didn't lose his head. He even saw a chance of cheating the other man, and no doubt he enjoyed the thought. He picked up the camera, took out the film, and gave it to Charles, laughing inwardly, since he knew the only photograph on that film was one of Miss Lethander, and he enjoyed the thought of Charles's reaction when he eventually made *that* discovery, and also the thought that all those delicious Gittan photographs were still in his own briefcase."

Durell stopped again and waited for some comment.

"Maybe it was like that," she said. "You know best, I suppose. I'm waiting for the *hypothesis*—how *I* come into the picture."

He sighed, a troubled sigh that she no doubt took as an attack of weakness and uneasiness on his part. But he ignored the way in which she took it.

"This is where you come in," he said. "You're the third visitor—and third time lucky. You knock on the door. Very quietly and cautiously, you knock on the door, so as not to arouse anyone's attention. When he answers, you go in. I imagine he was much more surprised to see you than his earlier visitors—what do you think?"

She laughed slightly ironically, almost arrogantly.

"It's possible," she said. "Victor wasn't one to be surprised much about things. He used to take things as they came. Go on, this interests me."

"As it should," he said. "And most of all, what should interest you is just *why* you had come."

"Ah, yes. Why had I come?"

"To get hold of a letter. The Stella letter."

There was a silence, a long silence, while Durell thought about how he should go on. At last he began hesitantly, as if feeling his way, his eyes fixed on her face to watch her reactions.

"Many years ago," he said, "there was a woman, and two men, who both loved her. She was married to one of them. The other was her lover. Such things don't last in the long run. The lover's daughter, for instance, happened to discover the relationship and the result was a trauma that was hard to heal, as well as a deep hatred for her father. The only thing that enabled her to bear it was the fact that her mother knew nothing about it, her brother knew nothing about it, and her sister knew nothing about it."

"But her mother had some idea, perhaps?"

He allowed her comment to float in the air, but he could not avoid hearing the bitterness.

"But one person who thought she knew," he went on, "was an old lady in this house. One week in August, six years ago, she summoned them to settle matters. She was a powerful old lady because she had money. Anyone who did not please her could easily be disinherited. And anyone who did not come at her summons could easily fall from grace. She also had that fine old quality of wanting to settle things without involving outsiders. She valued the reputation of the family very highly. She loathed scandals. Although she had probably been disappointed many times on that point, she considered it self-evident that the family should stick together, that whatever happened within the family had nothing whatever to do with anyone else. Since she was head of the family, she liked to take things in her own hands, put them right, arrange things, and give the directives she felt best and most appropriate from the point of view of her matriarchal assumptions. People obeyed her because she had money."

He fell silent again, waiting for a comment, but Vera said nothing. Durell had the impression she was waiting tensely for the next installment.

"So this old lady summoned them here, six years ago. But things did not work out as she had planned. Stella was not the kind of person to allow herself to be steered by someone else, however much money was involved. That led to Stella's death. Stella was murdered. Stella was thrown down the ancestral precipice."

"By whom? The old lady?"

"No." Durell smiled mysteriously. "But the old lady knew who had done it. When the two men had returned to their respective homes, the old lady wrote a letter to one of them, and from that letter it is clear who the murderer was . . ."

He paused dramatically, watching for her reaction. But Vera said nothing, just waited expressionlessly for him to go on.

"Martin had that letter," he said. "Victor happened to see it on some occasion and drew his own conclusions at once. He also realized the letter contained infinite possibilities for anyone who knew how to exploit it in the right way. He also appeared to think he was chosen to do so. So he took the letter. Time went by. Eventually it happened. Victor had gotten himself into such a mess that the only way out was to exploit the letter."

"And that's where I come into the picture again."

"Exactly. You don't think that letter ought to be exploited. In fact, you're determined to stop it and to get the letter. You take a gun with you to force him into handing it over. And you're clever enough to be wearing gloves so as not to leave a calling card. Not only that, *you want not only the letter but also the certainty that the contents of the letter will be destroyed.* That involved a death sentence for Victor— even if he gives you the letter—and not only for him but for Martin, too—and not only for those two but also for Miss Lethander. *For them all, the letter has become the lowest common denominator.*"

She gasped. During the next long pause he saw that she was pale and shaken, but she nodded faintly and whispered to him to go on.

"As far as Victor and Martin were concerned, you had your

plan arranged. It was to appear and be interpreted as murder
—the motive blackmail—and suicide—the motive anguished
regret. As far as Miss Lethander was concerned—suicide—the
motive grief, the scandal, the pointlessness of going on living.
Explaining the motive would not be difficult. Nor would explaining *how* it had happened from case to case. The only
thing to be done was to ensure that the *technique* was right,
was logical and acceptable, isn't that so?"

She nodded again.

"Now, then—you go into his room," Durell went on. "You
see the gun already lying there on the table and that shakes
you up slightly. Supposing he picks it up and uses it on *you*
when he learns what you're after? Could it be that he was
even *expecting* you? Naturally you make some comment
about the gun because that is what any visitor would do on
seeing a pistol lying on the table. Perhaps he told you the
whole story about Charles and his amusement at the thought
of Charles's face when he saw what kind of film he had acquired. While he was telling his story you decided to vary
your original plan somewhat. True, you had your own gun in
your bag all ready for use, but perhaps there was a certain
risk he would have time to pick up his gun before you managed to get yours out, or that it would all end in a duel, or
that with a gun in his hand he would refuse to turn over
what you had come to get. The variation was to be that you
would use *his* gun instead of your own. So you laughed at
the story about how Victor had tricked Charles, at the same
time picking up his gun in your gloved hand, and when that
was done, you stopped laughing and pointed it at him, saying
that you really meant it and he might as well hand over the
letter. Then Victor turned pale. He realized that you really
did mean it, and he got out the letter and gave it to you."

"Where was the letter?" she asked breathlessly, not allowing a single detail in his account to slip by.

"I'd like to take a qualified guess and say he simply had it
on him—in his pocket," said Durell. "And if you ask me why

I think that, it's because I presume he never got out of the chair during your visit, and we found no sign whatever of either the room or the briefcase or his suitcase having been searched. And because you would certainly not have fired the gun until you had the letter in your hand. Do you think that sounds plausible?"

She nodded slowly but did not reply.

"So he took out the letter and gave it to you. And when that was done—you fired."

She gasped again and whispered, "And then I fired."

Durell looked at her gravely. He couldn't help noticing she was so deeply involved that the whole scene was being enacted before her with all the intense mental stress that entailed.

"You'll probably protest that it's incredible that you'd dare fire a gun in a room next to Martin's. The house is certainly well built and not thin-walled, but *Martin* could hardly help hearing it. No, he couldn't—*if he'd been in there*. But he wasn't. And you knew he wasn't there because you knew where he was. We'll come back to that . . . Now, then—you're in Victor's room and Victor is lying dead on the floor. You put the gun in your bag and look at the letter, and you discover something very unpleasant. It's not the original. It's a photographic copy of the letter you want. Perhaps you should have foreseen that possibility. You know Victor is a skilled photographer and always had his camera handy. When he happens to see the letter in the drawer in Martin's desk, naturally it makes sense to photograph it rather than take the original, for if Martin were to discover the letter was missing, there'd be hell to pay. Well—this discovery forces you to modify your plan yet again. You must get hold of the original *before* you can go any further.

"You left the room, locked it on the outside, and put the key in your pocket. Then, presumably, you sat in the hall waiting for your father. He came eventually and you asked to speak to him, and then you went into his room. I imagine you now did three things before negotiations started. First, you wanted his fingerprints on the gun, so you took it out of your bag and gave it to him, telling him that Victor had asked you to give it to him—or that you'd found it somewhere in the house and thought he ought to be a little more careful about leaving guns about like that—it doesn't matter what you thought up. He took it and put it down on the table by the window. Second, you managed to smuggle the key to Victor's room into his dressing-gown pocket. How would I know? Perhaps you went up to him and hugged him to create the opportunity. Third, I think you put some more wood on the fire to keep the cauldron boiling while you both took a trip in the car to get the original letter from the manor. For that little improvisation was what you had to do . . ."

He stopped again and looked at her.

"Any objections?" he said.

Vera tried to say something, but her voice got stuck in her throat. She cleared her throat.

"How could I get Martin to agree to that?" she said slowly. "Do you really think he would—"

"Yes," said Durell abruptly. "Yes, I do. You had a very effective means of persuasion that he dared not defy. You threatened him with Miss Lethander. If he didn't give you that letter, so that you could destroy it, then you'd go to Miss Lethander and tell her that Martin had kept her letter—for god knows what evil purpose—and if the purpose was what you believed, then Miss Lethander, upright self-appointed judge over the family that she was, would disinherit Martin."

"So you think you know what purpose Martin had in mind when he kept that letter?" She sounded surer now, almost ironic.

"Yes."

"Perhaps you'd tell me."

"Yes. I'll come back to that—but let's go on for the moment."

He drew a deep breath and continued. "Martin agreed to

get the letter and give it to you. But I imagine he pointed out at the same time that Victor had a copy, and that it probably wouldn't be easy to get him to part with it. Then you smiled. 'Yes,' you said. 'He will for fifteen thousand kronor. You'll buy that copy for fifteen thousand kronor and then you'll give it to me.' It was indeed a tricky game you were playing— one that truly required a poker face."

He laughed somewhat harshly before going on. "So you drove over to the manor in the greatest secrecy, with no head-lights on, because discretion was of mutual interest to you both. Martin went in and got the letter, but in the turbu-lence of the moment he left his keys behind on the desk. Then you came back here.

"What happened now? You went back to his room with him. You were given the letter and you put it in the fire, which was now quite low. Perhaps you stayed for a while to watch for the right moment—the right moment from several points of view—to continue with the diabolical arrangement, carried out in a second, which was to assure his presumed suicide. While you were still there, Martin having said he was tired, perhaps a little drunk, and would like to go to bed, the treacherous carbon monoxide started seeping into the room."

He paused again and looked straight at her, but before she had time to say anything, he started again. "You left Martin. He locked the door behind you. He even shot the little bolt on the inside to ensure no one would take him by surprise. Then he lay down on the bed and thought, perhaps with a slight headache and feeling dizzy—but that was the drink, of course, and the start of a hangover . . . A few min-utes later he would be dead, as carbon monoxide works swiftly and imperceptibly, as well as fatally. The discovery is made in the morning. Actually, it was highly likely that all these machinations and your artfully implemented plan would have succeeded, although a few question marks re-mained—that the damper was actually open, for instance, and the carbon-monoxide poisoning puzzling. On the other hand, it *was* possible that Martin had closed the damper in order to end his life, then regretted it and opened it again, not realizing the air was already so deadly that he would die anyway. As I said, it could have succeeded.

"But what inevitably revealed a different course of events was the gun—your great fatal mistake with the gun. You discovered it yourself, but it was already too late by then. It doesn't matter whether you discovered it when you went back to your room that night or whether it was in the morning before the police had been called. The evidence was locked in with Martin and inaccessible. Your mistake was that you'd left the *wrong* gun with Martin. Not the one you'd used on Victor—Martin's own pistol, that is—but the one you'd brought with you in your bag. I can imagine your desperation. Well—there was still one chance. For even if the conclusion had by then been drawn that this was two murders, it could be arranged for the wrong murderer to be caught. There was one poor wretch who would be certain to be suspected almost immediately, and that was Charles. He was beside himself with jealousy. He'd been in Victor's room —you knew that. He'd threatened him with a gun. He'd got hold of the film. His fingerprints—thank goodness—must be on the gun you still had in your bag. How would he be able to prove that he had only threatened Victor with the gun, not fired it?"

Durell stopped again and waited to see what Vera's reaction would be. There was none. She was standing as still as a statue over by the wall, and her silence encouraged him to continue.

"All day, you thought about how you could carry out your new plan, and gradually the contours grew clearer. You even found that the third act—the original composition—did not need reworking. On the contrary, it would be easily integrated despite the cadenza *ad libitum* you were now forced to carry out. It so happened you had good reason to suspect there might be yet *another* copy of that fatal letter, and that copy was in Miss Lethander's keeping. You knew the old lady well. You knew she usually wrote her letters in pencil so she could make a carbon copy of what she had written. And you knew she kept her correspondence in a file . . . And now, my dear, I'm going to do a little guessing.

"I think you went into Miss Lethander's room to search for that copy in her file. But I don't think it was *there* because, after all, this letter was six years old. You knew perfectly well Miss Lethander also kept some old papers in the *attic*, and with any luck the copy would be there, *if* she'd made a copy of the letter as she usually did. Well, you waited until the evening—rather late, too. You took a flashlight and slipped up to the attic. It was intelligent of you to take a flashlight because someone might have noticed—old Miss Lethander, for instance, who might well have gone past the attic door even at that hour—and also someone might have noticed the light on the stairs, and it could also have been so dark up there you would need a light. Who knows, the bulb might even have been dead. So you went up there without switching any lights on, taking the pistol with you, of course. Then you went into the dressing room, where those old files were kept. You could risk putting that light on.

"Then suddenly it happens. Someone turns a light on in the attic. Someone is coming up the stairs. You quickly put the file back, reach up and loosen the bulb, then hide among the clothes. Then you see it's Veronica. She tries to switch on the light, but it doesn't work. But she takes a few garments in the semidarkness, leaves the room, and goes into the corner room to look at them. That gives you your opportunity. You've decided the gun *must* be put in the corner room because you figure that's the room they'll examine thoroughly, and you *must* be sure it's found. Perhaps you even *know*, or have concluded, that Charles was spying on Gittan and Victor up there, and he may have left prints outside—or why not actually *inside* the room?

"While Veronica is in the corner room you slip out and

into the shadows beyond, waiting for an opportunity. It comes almost at once. She was dissatisfied with her first choice of garments. She goes back into the dressing room to try some more. But she *must* have more light. Then it occurs to her that perhaps the bulb isn't dead, just loose, so she gets up on a box, tightens it, and there you are—it *works*. What does she do then? And what do you do? *She* takes a couple of dresses and goes back into the corner room. Meanwhile *you've* slunk into the corner room and put the pistol in the desk, then slipped back into the shadows again. I don't really need to recapitulate what happened next. After you blacked out the attic and dazzled Veronica with the flashlight, paralyzing her with terror, you slipped out into the corridor, put the flash-light outside the attic door downstairs, and made your way unseen out of the house.

"At last you could breathe freely again. Despite this dangerous intermezzo, your improvised cadenza had been successfully completed, perhaps even strengthening the already considerable suspicions against Charles. An even more logical conclusion than that the pistol had just been hidden would be that the murderer had been up there to *get* it—and to remove the incontrovertible fingerprint-covered evidence the pistol constituted . . ."

Once again he stopped and studied her face. She was pale and staring intently back at him.

"But you just think all that," she said suddenly. "Bertil—you don't know, do you? They're just hypotheses—you've no evidence."

He snorted.

"Both," he said. "Both hypotheses and evidence. They're hypotheses until the guilty person confesses."

"And you imagine, of course, that the guilty person will confess. Poor Bertil . . ."

He pretended not to notice the faint undertone of defiance —or perhaps doubt—in her voice, and went on relentlessly. "Presumably you never had time to find out whether that copy of the letter was in the attic or not. I don't think it was there. Because I happen to know Miss Lethander wrote that particular letter in ink—she neither wanted nor needed a copy . . . Well, you didn't know what, but I think you eventually decided that that particular copy—if it existed—was far too important, to Miss Lethander, too, not to be kept in her room. For what you could *not* make out from the photocopy was whether Miss Lethander had written in ink or pencil. Let me continue. We're now coming to the events of yesterday . . ."

He drew a deep breath, then started again. "You went into old Miss Lethander's room after her midday nap. You chose exactly the right moment, since you did not wish to be disturbed, and that meant you had to wait until Alma Gren had taken Miss Lethander her usual sleeping pill. You were very familiar with the old lady's habits. But what you didn't know was that yesterday Alma had to take up another pill because Miss Lethander had kindly given the first one to poor, nervous Ulla Svensson. What you also couldn't possibly foresee was that Fredrik Svensson would barge right into the middle of one of the most dramatic phases of this course of events.

"But now, my dear, it is no longer a question of hypotheses, but one of clear, logical reasoning. Listen carefully. The very fact that Miss Lethander let you in sealed her fate. Your aim was, as I said before, not only to destroy the letter and any possible copies but also to wipe out *all knowledge of its contents*. And Miss Lethander knew. I imagine even Miss Lethander knew, or at least had some idea, that you might be guilty of the murder of both Victor and Martin—but that's irrelevant in this context. For you it was still necessary to carry the whole game to its logical conclusion. Perhaps you asked her about the copy of the letter. Perhaps she gave it to you. Perhaps she said there was no copy of that letter, with its troublesome contents—so compromising that no copy should exist. Well—you opened the window and threw Miss Lethander out. Perhaps you hit her first—how would I know? But

Miss Lethander fell down the ancestral precipice, the triple murder was complete, and the odds were very good.

"In *this* case the final conclusion should be clear. Miss Lethander had taken her own life, old and tired as she was, disappointed, full of grief, not even her money helping to keep the family together—perhaps even the possibility of inheritance bringing on the tragedy. For you there remained only to produce *technical* evidence that it was suicide, which meant disappearing from the room, locking the door behind you, and later, when Miss Lethander was found, making sure you had an opportunity to slip the key into her pocket. Actually, that was not entirely necessary. If you had no opportunity to put the key in her pocket, you could also have thrown it down the ravine so that it was found in the same place as Miss Lethander had been found—no doubt you'd thought that out. But chance struck in the form of Fredrik Svensson.

"Listen carefully, now. Before you had time to leave the room, someone suddenly knocked on the door. You must have gone rigid with fright. You simply could not be discovered at that moment, in that place. Like a cat, you slipped into Miss Lethander's bedroom and waited, hardly daring to breathe, I imagine. You heard Fredrik come in, a little drunk, heard him rummaging around and then come toward the bedroom door. Perhaps you even saw him through the crack, looking in, hesitating over whether he dared go into the holy of holies, and then slowly, muttering a little, I should think, leaving Miss Lethander's apartment again. Just as you did a minute later. And thus everything was completed."

Durell fell silent, staring at her, trying to lure some protest out of her, to get her to point out sarcastically the weaknesses in his case, or perhaps even dismiss it all as eccentric fantasies with little or no evidence that would convince a court. No protests were forthcoming, but *she* was. She walked quietly and calmly over to him and sank into the chair opposite.

"I'd like to ask a few questions. May I?"

"Of course."

"What kind of diabolical arrangement did I use to poison Martin?"

"A balloon," said Durell, smiling slightly wearily. "Balloons are like soap bubbles—they rise and fall. You had a balloon in your bag when you went into Martin's room. You blew it up in there and knotted the mouth, as is usually done with balloons. When Martin had his back turned, you put it into the open fireplace and the hot air took it up the flue until it covered the opening exactly like a cork in a bottle. The trap was laid—immediately, unnoticeably, fatally. A long time after Martin was dead and the embers were no longer producing enough heat to keep the balloon up, although they were still glowing slightly—not until then did the balloon start to sink, leaving the flue free for the carbon monoxide to blow away during the hours to follow. It sank right down into the fire and the remaining embers burst and consumed it. Most of it was destroyed, but a few fragments remained. That didn't matter much. Pieces of burst balloons had already been put in that fire earlier that evening. We noticed later there was some ash and a few fragments of paper *outside* the fireplace, which could have been an indication that something had exploded in the fire. But, my god, to draw that conclusion *then*—when there was a multitude of much more plausible explanations."

"Do you know all this?"

"Yes, I experimented beforehand. The bang from the balloon bursting was what you heard in Martin's room when I was in there—not a shot."

He paused briefly.

"And as I said," he went on, putting emphasis on each word, "that explosion also shattered an alibi. Charlotte and John heard a shot at twenty past two during Sunday night. But that wasn't a pistol shot they heard—it was the balloon bursting. But Alma Gren—*she* heard a pistol shot. And it was *one* o'clock then. Unfortunately no one heard *both* shots, but one group heard the one shot and the other the other shot. If anyone had heard *both* shots, we would probably have gotten to the truth considerably earlier."

He looked at her and smiled hesitantly. "If we now continue the game—how did you dare take the risk of someone hearing the shot? Shall I take a guess? First of all, you didn't figure on the balloon making such a loud bang. Second, you hadn't figured on the visit to the manor. And third, perhaps you didn't think it was a risk at all. Who on earth would believe it really *was* a shot? And if someone did, who would get up in the middle of the night to find out if it was? No, the significance of that bang in the night would not dawn on anyone until they found the victim."

He paused again and gazed thoughtfully past her, out into the room.

"One more thing," he said suddenly. "That alibi—in some way you found out that Alma had heard a shot at one o'clock, whereas Charlotte and John said it was at twenty past two. The first time was dangerous—but the second would actually give you a marvelous alibi because at twenty past two in the morning you were in your room and could prove it. So on Sunday morning you simply went to the kitchen, stopped the kitchen clock, and put the hands at one o'clock. Abracadabra —the clock had been stopped all the time. Alma's testimony was useless, and she, poor thing, was the first to admit that she'd made a mistake, for John and Charlotte's information was irrefutably reliable. So it was obvious that Victor had died at twenty past two in the morning."

Vera stared at him.

"That was an excellent account, Bertil," she said. "But it all sounds fantastic. Isn't the motive a little feeble?"

"Why? It depends how strong emotions are in a daughter, I imagine—vis à vis a father—and how long she is prepared to go on protecting him. You have no idea how many motives a policeman can find infinitely less well substantiated than those in this case."

"And where was Martin when I shot Victor?"

"With Mauritz."

"Uh-huh," she said, sounding tired. "Shall we stop playing this game now?"

"No, not yet. There is just one more question I expected you to ask. *Why* did Martin keep that letter? He must have had some purpose. I think I can account for that. Listen, now, my dear. Six years ago Stella was thrown down the ancestral precipice, exactly as Miss Lethander was yesterday. Mauritz did it, and both Miss Lethander and Martin knew that Mauritz had done it. As far as Miss Lethander was concerned, the matter was perfectly settled—she would remain as silent as the grave. But things weren't quite so settled for Martin. I would also say that Martin tried to blackmail Mauritz—for no doubt Martin was in chronic need of money. So let's presume that perhaps not all that long after Stella's death he wrote to Mauritz with the intention of selling his silence. You happened to read that letter, and you hid its contents in the depths of your heart, and from that day onward, you knew how Stella had died. What did Mauritz do? He turned to Miss Lethander and told her about the attempted blackmail. And what do you think Miss Lethander did? She wrote to Martin. She made it clear to him that if he didn't forget the whole Stella affair, he could count on being written out of her will."

He paused, looking challengingly at her.

"Are you with me?"

She nodded.

"That letter he had from Miss Lethander," he went on, "became his most valuable possession. With its help he could one day, after Miss Lethander had gone and he'd had his share of her estate—with its help he could go back to Mauritz and start blackmailing him all over again. But not until then —not until then. *You* realized that. And *you*, one of Miss Lethander's confidantes—you'd begun to suspect that old Aunt Lethander had little desire to go on living much longer. Over the years, or perhaps more recently, but definitely since you'd heard through the wall Martin threatening Mauritz and demanding fifteen thousand kronor immediately for the copy of the letter Victor had—which was just as dangerous to Mauritz as to his own expectations of Miss Lethander's will—you swiftly decided to implement your plans. A murder, which would have to be a double murder, and to make quite sure, a triple murder. I realize that events and plans may have developed at a tremendous speed. Supposing you had planned to murder Martin in peace and quiet —just as it was carried out. At that moment the whole family was together in the house. Then you suddenly learn that Victor also knows about the Stella letter. Maybe he even boasted about it when you were dancing at Miss Lethander's party—how would I know? But, anyhow, you took the consequences."

He fell silent and again looked challengingly at her.

"Well?"

But she was silent, and he became impatient.

"Admit it now," he said. "Don't you agree it's actually enough to speculate one's way logically through to what that damned Stella letter contained, and then everything becomes as clear as crystal—can't you admit that?"

"Yes, perhaps I can," she said almost sorrowfully. "May I stop playing this game now? I'm too tired to go on trying to imagine it was me. But *if* it had been me and you'd set it all out like that, and if I'd been her, then I'd have given up. I wonder whether she had to stand on tiptoe to reach the light bulb?"

She fell silent and there was a brief pause before she went on.

"So I was supposed to be Malin?" she said.

"Yes—that's it. You were to be the murderer. If you think it holds water—then so do I."

He gave her a look of admiration.

"It'd be good if we could go on meeting—later on, I mean, when all this is over."

EPILOGUE

Miss Lethander did not have a copy of the letter, neither in the file in her desk nor up in the attic. After Malin had confessed and confirmed that almost everything had happened as Durell had deduced, she also told him she had borrowed the gun she had at first thought of using from her husband, Sergej, who always carried a gun on him because, though not a member, he felt threatened by Ustasja. Then, of her own accord, she had given Durell the copy she had forced out of Victor, and which for some obscure reason she had not been able to bring herself to destroy. The letter, in Miss Lethander's elegant style, ran:

DEAR MARTIN:

I am an old woman and I have seen much evil in my life. I also know much of it has to happen, and that it is often preferable to keep *silent* than let it happen again—happen to people close to one and of whom one should be fond. You know as well as I do who pushed Stella over the precipice. But do not use that knowledge, for as God is my judge your guilt is in fact the greater. *Forget* all this. Then the world will also forget it. But if you do anything ill considered, I will disinherit you and yours.

YOUR AUNT LETHANDER